The Top Ten Ways *to* Love Your Wife

Hans and Donna Finzel

Faith Marriage is an imprint of
Cook Communications Ministries, Colorado Springs, Colorado 80918
Cook Communications, Paris, Ontario
Kingsway Communications, Eastbourne, England

THE TOP TEN WAYS TO LOVE YOUR WIFE
© 2001 by Hans and Donna Finzel

First Printing 2001
Printed in the United States of America

1 2 3 4 5 6 7 8 9 1 0 Printing/Year 05 04 03 02 01

Editor: Craig Bubeck, Sr. Editor
Cover Design: Maurine R. Twait
Interior Design: Maurine R. Twait
Cover Photo: Andy Caulfield

Unless otherwise noted, Scripture quotations are taken from the Holy Bible: New
International Version. Copyright © 1973, 1978, 1984 by International Bible Society.
Used by permission of Zondervan Publishing House. All rights reserved.

Library of Congress Cataloging-in-Publication Data

Finzel, Hans.
  [Top ten ways to drive your wife crazy and how to avoid them]
  The top ten ways to love your wife / by Hans and Donna Finzel.
     p. cm.
Previously published as: The top ten ways to drive your wife crazy and
how to avoid them.
Includes bibliographical references.
  ISBN 0-7814-3739-3
  1. Husbands--United States. 2. Wives--United States--Psychology. 3.
Marriage--United States. 4. Marriage--Religious aspects--Christianity.
I. Finzel, Donna. II. Title.
  HQ756 .F56 2001
  646.7'8--dc21
                        2001005611

If you are a husband who wants a marriage that rates a 10 on the richter scale of holy matrimony, then Hans and Donna Finzel's book is a must read . . . and must do for you!

—*Dr. E. Glenn Wagner, author and*
Senior Pastor, Calvary Church, Charlotte, NC

Hans and Donna Finzel know what they are talking about. *Ten Ways* is one of those books that actually says what ten other books have only been trying to say. Here is a book for those who are either preparing for the commitment of marriage, struggling in a marriage relationship, or simply want to improve what God has blessed for many years. This book makes my "top ten" list for anyone needing an injection of romance and love in their marriage.

—*Dr. Glen Martin, Senior Pastor,*
Community Baptist Church, Manhattan Beach, CA

Dedication

To our parents

ↄ Mark and Anita Bubeck

ↄ Alfred and Brigitte Finzel

Thanks for your lifelong examples of the beauty
of what marriages are meant to be.

Foreword

Introduction

References Cited

oreword

Some of you have picked up this book thinking to yourself, *Great! Here are some new ideas on love-making techniques. We could use some creative input!* That is not exactly what this book is all about. To be sure, mastering the art of loving one another in a healthy marriage relationship can lead to all kinds of fun in the bedroom! But ironically, much about what makes for a great love life happens outside of the bedroom walls—it's the day-to-day routine of a marriage, and avoiding the notorious pitfalls, that can make or break you as a lover.

This summer, as we (Hans and Donna) write these pages, we are attending several weddings. Have you noticed how much people are spending on weddings? The cost of a decent wedding these days is outlandish, but people spare no expense for their special day. One day! But what about the investment in the days that follow? Sadly, it seems that weddings are more important than marriages in our country.

In this day of throwaway marriages, we want to have a marriage that will last a lifetime and be a solid example to our four children. We want our family to be a force for good in this culture that is losing the hope of lifelong marriage. As we launch our kids into adulthood, our prayer is that they will find mates who are committed to fulfilling the vow at the altar, 'till death do us part. We know this is a monumental expectation, especially in this day and age; but what an infinitely worthy goal!

Some of you are just getting started in your marriages. We are glad to have your attention. Others of you are living in a marriage that is not the relationship you dreamed of as a young person. You live with disappointment, boredom, and unfilled needs. Of course, some of you reading these pages have already failed in a relationship or two. We trust our words help as you forget the past and look to a better tomorrow, working in God's grace toward a resurrection of hope for your marriage.

Then there are you long-termers who are making a good run at your marriage and are looking for a refresher course. This book can give you the encouragement and fresh ideas about how to make marriage work in the twenty-first century. It may be old fashioned, but it's a tried and true promise from Scripture that God honors the couples who are committed to making it work for a lifetime.

We share with you our experiences and lessons learned from 25 years of a marriage that is far from perfect, but one that we have enjoyed. When we stood at that altar in suburban Chicago in 1975, we vowed to be committed to Jesus Christ as our Savior, and to make Him an essential part of our home. We want you, the reader, to be clear that this book is written with that foundation in mind. We look to the Bible as the guide for having a marriage that will work as God designed it. Despite common misperceptions, the Bible is very practical and has much to say about men and women, families, and marriage.

We also share with you from the lives and marriages of dozens of other couples. The list we came up with for the *Top Ten Ways to Love Your Wife* was gleaned from their input. We want to acknowledge and thank all of those couples who contributed their real-life stories to this book.

Introduction

Once upon a time there was a little blond girl named Donna, who grew up in a family of all girls in the beautiful state of Colorado. She had a warm, loving family and decided she would marry her daddy when she grew up—a dream of many a young daughter before reality sets in.

Finally, the day came when Donna realized that she really couldn't marry her dad, so she said to her parents, "Well, then, when I get married, we'll get a trailer and live in our backyard!"

Meanwhile, a little German boy named Hans was growing up in another world. He was the first-generation son of immigrants from the old country, who had landed in Huntsville, Alabama. His dad was busy building rockets to put the United States on the moon.

Hans never met Donna growing up in Alabama. And he never heard about the business of the trailer in the backyard . . . until later.

As God would have it, in His amazing grand scheme of things, Donna and Hans both ended up as college students in Columbia, South Carolina, in the early 1970s. Hans was a senior the year Donna entered as a freshman at Columbia International University. They fell in love, and soon Hans felt it was time to ask Donna's father for her hand in marriage.

On a hot August Saturday in Chicago, Hans finally got up the courage to ask Mark Bubeck for his daughter's hand in marriage. The two decided to meet at the church Mark pastored in Oak Park, Illinois. Of all places, the fateful moment came while sitting and talking on the steps in front of the sanctuary, right by the altar. Hans, experiencing more than just a little sense of unworthiness, felt as if he were asking Moses, the holy man, if he could marry one of his daughters.

"I would like to ask your permission to marry Donna," Hans finally blurted out. With a straight face Pastor Bubeck replied, "I ask just two things of you, Hans. First, I want you to be sure in your heart that this is truly God's will for the two of you. And second, I want you to buy a trailer and live in our backyard." Sensing the panic on Hans' face, he burst into a big smile and filled him in on the family joke about Donna's trailer.

That was over 25 years ago, and from the vantage point of time it does seem almost a fairy tale story. We never did buy the trailer, but we learned quickly that you do get more than a spouse in the marriage deal. You marry into families that have unique cultures and ways of doing things. And you bring your families' values and views into your marriage as you blend both backgrounds into a new hybrid—one with its own set of flaws and shortcomings.

One thing that has carried us through all the speed bumps and potholes of our marriage, is the belief that God brought the two of us together back then in blissful college days; and He is just as much keeping us together in present. We are committed alongside Him to keep our marriage vows that we recited the following summer in that same sanctuary in Oak Park.

The Top Ten Ways to Love Her

More to the point, the question a lot of you husbands are asking is, *How do I love my wife for the long haul, but still in a way that means something to her?* No matter how much we wish it were otherwise, we all learn well by trial and error. I, Hans, have found this to be true in the business of leadership; and I have similarly learned how to love Donna best by practicing this same principle: If you don't understand how you do it wrong, you'll never know how to do it right. To understand what I'm doing wrong has meant my choosing to being vulnerable, open to feedback, and constantly going against the flow in a world that is quick to give up on marriage. Our constant prayer is "Lord, may we never become just another sad statistic."

Let's repeat the principle again:

> *If you don't understand how you do it wrong,*
> *you'll never know how to do it right.*

The top ten ways to love your wife become real and personal as you experience each "way" through trial and error. We need to know that it takes time—a lifetime of work. Relationships are always slipping and sliding because we are two human beings joined together. We're not looking for perfection here; we are looking for positive, growing, nurturing marriages that can be as fun as when you first got married . . . perhaps even better!

Anything but a Put-Down

So who would want to read this book anyway? Wives buying it for their husbands and leaving it on his nightstand might not be a bad approach. Maybe he just might get the idea that he could learn something. But how about you husbands out there? All you need is to rack up more guilt points, right? Well, this book is not about guilt.

This book is not a put-down on men. It *is* a fresh glimpse into how most women are wired and how their men can run with, not against those currents. These pages are meant to be an "upper," revealing positive ways for men and women to understand how opposites can live together in a warm, growing, building relationship for a lifetime.

If we can agree that all marriages are made up of essential opposites—one man and one woman, and therein a world of difference—then we are well on the road to success.

As the man in our marriage, I have come to learn that the key to making Donna happy and our marriage last—and prosper—is to really work at understanding this female person I live with. In fact, I tell my three sons repeatedly when they cannot figure out some action or feelings of their sister or mom: "Listen, guys, the study of women will be a lifelong pursuit for you. You'll never get to the bottom of the complex nature of the female heart. But try as best you can to learn all you can. It's worth it."

Are You Getting the Message?

Peter Jennings reported on the evening news one night that in the past 24 years the divorce rate has multiplied fivefold in the United States. From the 1970s through the 1990s the number of divorces shot up from 4 million to 20 million. Clearly these are epidemic proportions!

Maybe you are a husband who feels your marriage is just fine. Still, your wife keeps saying she wants you to "do something!" She may be expressing a cry for "help" that is deeper than you imagine. Have you ever taken the time to really study her? Consider this quote from Gary Smalley:

> Who would think of allowing an untrained man to climb into the cockpit of an airplane and tinker with the gauges? Or who would allow a novice to service the engines of a modern jet? Yet we expect men to build strong, loving

relationships without any education at all. A man must be 'educated': He first must discover the essentials of genuine love, then practice them until his skills are sharp and natural (*If Only He Knew*, Gary Smalley, pp. 29-30).

Just when I think I'm getting the hang of truly understanding Donna . . . hubcaps.

It Was a Dark and Foggy Night

Who would expect that the insignificant things tend to become the most significant cause of heat and friction between two civilized, married people? Probably anyone who has been married more than just a few short, blissful months—even a couple of years. Ah, but we who have been husbands a bit longer know all too well that it's those little foxes that strike hardest (see Song of Solomon 2:15).

It all started on a dark and foggy night on the back roads of Highway 20 in northern Illinois.

Hans' words, "insignificant things" are enough to illustrate the immense chasm that can exist between men's and women's perspective of the very same event! Let me (Donna) illustrate.

I was returning from speaking at a retreat in Iowa. I was utterly exhausted and spent, yet content and praising the Lord after a wonderful time of ministry and teaching on the New Age Movement. I was returning on Saturday evening in serious fog and rain. Driving on a winding, unnerving road, I had to concentrate hard just to see it. It felt as if I were in "the twilight zone" . . . the highway to nowhere! As a matter of fact, I was returning home at this time only because Hans had flown out a few hours earlier for ministry in Pennsylvania. Our four children were at home with a baby-sitter until I could get back to them. Hans had given me his cellular phone, which he had only recently received for his work.

After driving nearly three hours under those conditions, I was finally on a smooth and straight portion. Suddenly it felt as if I were losing my steering. Struggling to keep control, I came to a stop on the shoulder. There I was in the pitch dark along a lonely road in the rain and fog, in the middle of nowhere! Still in my dress clothes with no flashlight, I got out to check the tires, pounding them on the top. They seemed okay to me. I then called "911," but couldn't even tell them where I was. I prayed and phoned home, where the baby-sitter was only able to get a few phone numbers for me. Hans had not left a number where he could be reached!

I struggled with the normal fears of a woman alone at night on a deserted road. And I prayed that any truck hurdling down the road could see me in the fog and avoid flattening me. As I was praying for protection and wisdom, a woman pulled up alongside to ask if I needed help. She was able to tell me my general location so the police could begin their search to find me. I waited, prayed, and continued calling friends asking for their prayers.

It took well over an hour for a police officer to arrive. With his lights on the van, we discovered that the front right tire had "blown" and was badly damaged! He called a tow truck. Later, as the tow-truck driver was hooking up the van, he told me how "lucky" I was to have had such a severe blowout on the only smooth stretch of road along that highway. I knew it wasn't luck; it was God's protection!

We drove into the small town to his auto shop. The driver was friendly and allowed me to use the phone to try to somehow locate Hans. The van was equipped only with a small temporary tire, and it was impossible to get a new tire on Saturday night. We were still twenty-five miles from civilization in Rockford, Illinois, and another long drive from there to home in such weather. After finally reaching Hans, it was agreed that the only reasonable decision would be to have Dave, the driver, tow me all the way home.

On the journey home in that fog God had arranged a "divine appointment" with Dave. He was a young husband and father, and he asked me questions about my teaching on the New Age. He had never heard about a personal relationship with Christ but was very open and interested as I shared from my own life and the Bible. His wife's aunt, it turned out, is a high-level promoter and teacher for the New Age and lives in Oregon. We finally arrived safely at my home at midnight.

Now for the clincher: when Hans got home and saw that I was okay, his first thought turned to the car . . . what is this thing with men and their cars? He looked at the van sitting in the garage and asked, "Did you get the hubcap?"

I was absolutely floored! The hubcap? I could have been killed! I had sat in the dark alone for one and one-half hours struggling in exhaustion just to get home to the kids, and *all he cares about is the stupid hubcap! Men!*

A few months later, we were laughing about what—to say the least—turned into a major flare-up. (Okay, I, Hans, was trying to laugh, but the wounds were perhaps still a bit raw in Donna.) Then she asked me, "Hey, Mr. big shot author of *The Top Ten Mistakes Leaders Make,* why not write a book on the top ten mistakes that husbands make?" That challenge became the book in your hands, which we decided to affectionately title with the positive look beyond the mistakes: *The Top Ten Ways to Love Your Wife.*

That illustrates why I approach our life together with this strategy: to love Donna is to understand her heart and to relate to her as the unique feminine creature that she is. But even after twenty-five years at it, when I do something hurtful that wounds her spirit, I wonder if I have learned anything at all.

As you might have guessed, we draw some points from our own marriage pilgrimage—that's because we're always having to work at building a stronger marriage ourselves. Whatever else it is, marriage isn't something you master and then relax. In fact we have surveyed dozens of married couples, asking a series of simple questions to broaden our perspective on how men can really love their wives (more of that later). They generally agree—you're always working at it. Our desire in these pages is to bring you ten keys that will unlock some doors in your relationship, leading to a stronger marriage . . . which means a happier wife.

Hero Husbands We Know

I want to affirm Hans' earlier assurance: this book is not about indulging in husband-bashing. Sure, guys make mistakes, but no more than the wives. Be honest—no one is perfect, and every marriage is a lifelong work in progress.

Granted, throughout these pages we reveal some of the insensitive things guys can do to their wives. But we will also share positive examples of men who are doing a great job of loving their wives—husbands we can all learn from.

Each of our ten chapters highlights a "Hero Husband" whom we know. From former president of Columbia International University, Robertson McQuilken, to Christian recording artist Steve Green, and including our own dads, we'll give you inside views of men who have the right stuff. These guys—though none of them is a perfect husband or father—still do certain things that make their wives happy to be married. They have listened, learned, and do it right; and we honor them for their gallant attempts to remain forever their wives' true loves.

The Power of Love

Though I don't refer to it often enough, I keep a list on my Palm Pilot of all the things I can do for Donna. I know that first on the list (a literal list that I'll share with you later) is simply "affection." It's a funny thing, and an example of how she's so very different from me. As a woman, she flourishes when I actively pour out my sincere affection upon her. Like food, she seems to need it every day, but this food she can't get enough of—she'll never overdose on it. It reminds us both of the great words of Wynonna and Naomi Judd:

Give a Little Love
by Paul Kennerley, performed by the Judds
(Used with permission: Warner Brothers Music)

Well, you can buy a diamond ring and slip it on my hand,
Or put me on a big ole plane and fly me to a foreign land,
Show me rows of fancy clothes and say,
"Honey, you can take your pick,"
That would be mighty kind, but it ain't gonna' do the trick.

Give a little love, mmmmm a squeeze and a little kiss,
Give a little hug, mmmmm I want some more of this,
Take a little time, yea, and make a little fuss,
That's what a woman wants . . .
So give a little love.

A word of clarification before we begin. Throughout these pages we will tell you stories about people we know and the interesting things that have happened in their marriages. We want very much to protect their privacy. *So, many names have been changed for both husband and wife, to protect their privacy as they quietly go about trying to make their marriages work.* We thank them for their great input.

The perfect marriage is a myth, but if we share our victories and defeats, we can help each other make it work. You'll find our "Top Ten Tips" placed thoughtfully throughout these pages—they are small, practical methods that can strengthen each of our marriages. These tips have come from good books that have helped our marriages, from friends who have shared their victories with us, and of course from God's own Word. Every marriage that lasts for the long haul is a victory for God and a powerful force in the increasingly fractured world in which we live.

Chapter

1

What Women Want
"All She Needs Is Love"

Love covers a multitude of sins—cliche, perhaps, but boy does it apply to marriage. Whatever you neglect, guys, don't let it be love. It's the most obvious, and the most obviously overlooked.

Most men know that affection is the odds-on favorite for their wives. But knowing the importance of affection is one thing—giving it . . . that's what is tough.

Women have a deep-seated need for tenderness and focused affection—the type that a gentle-spirited, kind husband offers his wife. Okay, that's fine for the rare find out there. But what about the rest (the most) of us? What if tenderness is tough for you as a man? Exactly what is this affection that they seem to crave?

1 What Women Want
"All She Needs Is Love"

Mel Gibson's character finds the secret of what women want in a movie with the same name. As he goes about pursuing women selfishly, an accident gives him a taste of what he needs. An electrical shock zaps him into a zone where he can hear what the women around him are thinking. And what is it that Mel learns? What do women want? In a word, love. But not just any love (at least, not what he considers to be love)—they want a sacrificial, compassionate, "I think I know how you are feeling, and I'm trying to care" kind of love.

Obviously, no one could claim to know all about love in marriage. So wherever you are on the question of loving your wife, our pilgrimage in this first chapter is worthwhile.

The Beatles were right in the lyrics to one of their first hits, "All You Need Is Love." But as their lives often revealed even more plainly, the supposedly simple things in life can be so complex. When all the votes of women we surveyed are in, the results are predictable. Yes, "all they need is love." But while most men know this about their wives, it's the doing of what we know that's the trick.

A Simple Survey of Couples

When the two of us set out to write these pages, we thought ten seemed like a good round number. We put our lists together based on the twenty-five years of experience in our own marriage, then began to ask married friends for input from their own experiences. From that we developed a questionnaire, which we sent out across the country and then around the world.

The results that came back from everywhere were fascinating. No matter where couples live and regardless of their economic or social standings, there are remarkable threads that run through all marriages.

Among some of the highlights, we learned:

- People seem to have the same problems in their marriages, no matter how long they've been married.

- People tend to be more forgiving of each other the longer they have been married.

- No one has a perfect marriage.

- Husbands can actually be quite transparent and knowledgeable about inadequacies in their marriage.

- Wives can understand and be forgiving of inadequacies.

Without a doubt, once our research was in, the clear message was that being loved is the key. Perhaps you're thinking that was pretty obvious without the research. Granted, but the strong responses reaffirm not only the importance of love in a woman's heart, but the reality that the need often isn't being met.

One problem is, the word "love" is used for everything from "I love these nachos" to "of course I love you, honey." So why is this obvious and most popular concept still at the root of the needs of every marriage? Let's take a look at some responses.

One of the questions we asked the husbands in our survey was this:

The First Question for Husbands:

"What do you think is your wife's number-one need that you should fulfill?"

Here is a sampling of answers, which became a singularly constant chorus:

From the Midwest: "The greatest single need of my wife is to be loved. I guess Paul had it right in Ephesians 5!"

From the West Coast: "Two words sum up her greatest need— 'affection' and 'attention.'"

From acquaintances in the Southwest: "This question is a no-brainer for me. She needs my love, which means my encouragement by paying complete attention to her."

From Colorado: "She needs my continual love and acceptance."

And from California: "She needs to be cherished, not just through words (although they are critical), but through thought and deed."

This is just a sampling, but enough to see a steady call for love—especially in the form of affection—that comes

Top ***10*** *Tip*

Just Say "I Love You"

From a wife in Illinois:
"It may seem like a little thing to him, but I need to be told every day that he loves me. I just can't get enough of those three little words—the biggest three words in my heart's language."

through loud and clear. Unfortunately, though we had asked an equal amount of questions (three each) of wives and husbands, we found that the majority of our responses came back from women.

It's probably telling that many men are too busy for questionnaires, especially when the questions have to do with such an often-guilt-ridden topic as your own marriage relationship! Nevertheless, many men did respond, and we were thankful for the balance of perspective that they brought.

The Power of Love

Try this simple experiment. Using the word "love," think of a song that has this four-letter gem in it and sing it. Are you singing? Okay, now try to think of a second song. We can't hear you! Now go for a third. We guess that you had absolutely no problem coming up with your songs.

Isn't love amazing? It is, without a doubt, the theme of more songs that have been written than any other topic, bar none. And some of these songs that come to our minds so easily (too bad we can't remember more important stuff this easily) pack a solid punch. Yes, even country music, which happens to be in the camp of Hans' favorite types of songs.

Even if you are not a lover of country music, please give us a chance with this example. This is a good place to repeat the words of that great chorus from Wynonna and Naomi Judd. Look at these lyrics, study them, and hear what they say. Better yet, get the album and listen to their inspiration!

Give a Little Love
by Paul Kennerley, performed by the Judds
(Used with permission: Warner Brothers Music)

Well, you can buy a diamond ring and slip it on my hand,
Or put me on a big ole plane and fly me to a foreign land,
Show me rows of fancy clothes and say,
"Honey, you can take your pick,"
That would be mighty kind, but it ain't gonna' do the
trick.

Give a little love, hmm a squeeze and a little kiss,
Give a little hug, hmm I want some more of this,
Take a little time, yea, and make a little fuss,
That's what a woman wants . . .
So give a little love.

The first question we asked the wives was this:

The First Question for Wives:

*"Describe an action, attitude, or habit that your
husband practices that frustrates you or hin-
ders your relationship."*

One of the wives responding to our questionnaire opened her
heart wide for us and shared this anonymous insight about her
cries for love from her husband, who is actually quite a wonderful fellow:

First there is a lack of touch. I need to constantly remind
him to "pretend he likes me" (teasingly) by holding my

hand or putting an arm around me or a hug—his family was not very affectionate that way, so I don't take it personally. But I still crave the affection.

The more we listen to the basic needs of women, the more we understand the profound wisdom of Paul, a single man who nevertheless was given great understanding about the bond of marriage. Simply and directly, Paul exhorted in Ephesians 5 what God intended to be activity, not merely passive emotions: "Husbands love your wives."

Husbands Love Your Wives

Let's look at this classic New Testament marriage passage in the Book of Ephesians. Paul was lifting love to its highest level when in Ephesians 5, he told us husbands to love our wives as "Christ loved the church." The more we think about this biblical mandate, the more implausible it seems. Nevertheless, married love is to reflect in the home the relationship that Christ has to His bride, the church. Listen to Paul's words:

> *Husbands, love your wives, just as Christ loved the church and gave himself up for her to make her holy, cleansing her by the washing with water through the word, and to present her to himself as a radiant church, without stain or wrinkle or any other blemish, but holy and blameless. In this same way, husbands ought to love their wives as their own bodies. He who loves his wife loves himself (Eph. 5:25-28).*

The word used here in Ephesians for *love* is the word used in the New Testament for the highest form of love. It is not *eros*, which means mere affection, romantic attraction, or sexual passion (what the media usually thinks of when it sings about and displays human love between men and women). No, this is the

How Many Times Is Too Much?

from Jim Smith

"I will tell you something else I have learned about women. You cannot tell her too many times a day that you love her. I have never had a woman say to me, 'I've got a horrible problem. My husband will not quit telling me he loves me. He just bores me to tears with it. He tells me incessantly.' I do not think a woman can hear that too much, if it is a genuine expression of affection and love."

—From *Learning to Live with the One You Love*, Jim Smith, p. 163

word *agape*, the selfless sacrificial love that puts others' needs before one's own. This is that kind of love that caused Christ to come to earth in the first place to redeem us as His church.

In Warren Wiersbe's commentary on Ephesians, *Be Rich*, he highlights some of the most important reasons that God designed marriage. Among them:

- to meet mankind's *emotional needs:* "It is not good for man to be alone";
- to meet mankind's *social needs* to have children and continue the race;
- to meet man's and woman's *physical need* to fulfill their God-given desires; and
- to meet the *spiritual purposes* in marriage, as the husband and wife experience together the submission and the love of Christ.

If the husband takes this model seriously—the Christ and the church example—he will love his wife in these ways.

Again quoting Wiersbe:

He will love her sacrificially—if he is submitted to Christ and filled with the spirit, his sacrificial love will willingly pay a price that she might be able to serve Christ and glorify Him.

He will love her with a sanctifying love—to sanctify means 'to set apart,' and with this aspect of love their relationship is protected and set apart from others.

He will love her with a satisfying love—marriage is meant to be a mutually satisfying experience. Man is not just to get his own needs met, but to nurture a relationship that is truly mutually satisfying" (*Be Rich,* Warren Wiersbe, pp. 50-51).

So there is sound biblical reasoning for love being what women need the most. It's obviously a reason for why the New Testament admonitions focus upon husbands loving their wives. It may seem like restating the obvious, but to listen to wives from Maine to California, it is a modern-day problem for today's husbands as much or more than it has ever been.

Perhaps we husbands need the gentle prodding of the words spoken by Jesus Himself: "Now that you know these things, you will be blessed if you do them" (John 13:17).

Hero Husbands We Know

Donna and I have known Robertson and Muriel McQuilken for thirty years. We first met them before we were married, as young students at Columbia International University in Columbia, South Carolina. Robertson was president of the school, and Muriel was a very gifted woman of God who exercised many gifts in several directions, both around the school and in other venues.

Muriel McQuilken, in fact, played an important role in bringing the two of us together. Hans was a senior in 1974, and Donna was an incoming freshman. "I'm about to graduate and am unattached, so certainly the woman I will marry is not at this school," Hans reasoned. He and several of his friends were all leaders on the campus that year—unattached seniors about to go out into the world and leave their mark. Then one spring day in early 1974, Muriel pulled aside Hans and his three senior cohorts and said, "Men, there is no girl like a CIU girl. You better get busy and find one before you leave!"

Well, Muriel was half kidding and half serious. She did feel that we all four needed wives committed to God to stand by our sides as we went out to make our mark on the world. And she must have known that all four of us were already seeing and showing interest in certain women on campus. By graduation, all four us

Genuine Love

from Gary Smalley

"If a couple has been married for more than five years, any persistent disharmony in their marriage relationship is usually attributable to the husband's lack of genuine love" (*If Only He Knew,* p. 74).

had found our future mates! And now, all these years later, we still thank Muriel for giving us that gentle and wise shove that we needed.

Years later in the spring of 1986, Robertson and Muriel came to visit us in Vienna, Austria, where we were working with a ministry to Eastern Europe. We had great days together showing the two of them our adopted city. We noticed right away, however, that something was not right with Muriel. Her memory seemed to have gaps, and she would tell us the same stories repeatedly. We thought we knew what might be wrong but said nothing. Soon we would learn that our worst fears were true.

Muriel McQuilken had developed Alzheimer's disease, and today she lives with Robertson in their humble home in Columbia. She is unable to speak or care for herself. We have visited Robertson and Muriel several times in their home since this brutal disease incapacitated her, and we have been overwhelmed by Robertson's love. To sit and watch him feed her and care for her as if she were a newborn is a humbling experience—daily, in the mundane, we saw love in action from a husband to his wife who can no longer return the favor.

In 1990, Robertson stunned the evangelical Christian community by stepping down as president of Columbia International University because his wife needed full-time care. He stated that he wanted to give back to her some of the nurturing care she had provided him for so many years. Over the intervening decade, her condition has deteriorated, and Robertson has shown many of us deep insights into the mysteries of love in marriage.

It seemed amazing enough to all of us that Robertson McQuilken gave up his career to care for his wife. But even more significant is to see his constant and unfailing love for her each and every day as he cares for her, much the way a parent cares for a helpless newborn. The situation has deteriorated from bad to worse in terms of her ability to function. Among the many painful effects of this disease is loss of control of most of her bodily functions, and of course she no longer talks. Just recently I, Hans, was in the McQuilken home in Columbia for a lunch visit with Robertson. I'm simply amazed and profoundly challenged by his unfailing love for his life mate, who at this point lies in bed 24/7, with no normal communication or interaction.

How can he keep up this kind of commitment? How can you love when there is no payback in return? Listen to these recent words of insight from Robertson, one of our all-time most honored hero husbands. We all wonder how he doesn't get tired taking care of Muriel when he gets no reciprocation from her:

> Recently, a student wife asked me that. Cindi has sort of adopted us. As we sat at the kitchen table sipping coffee, she said, "Don't you ever get tired?"
>
> "Tired? Every night. That's why I go to bed."
>
> "No, I mean tired of . . ." and she tilted her head toward Muriel, who sat silently in her wheelchair, her vacant eyes saying, "No one at home just now." I responded to Cindi's question, "Why, no, I don't get tired. I love to care for her. She's my precious."
>
> "Well, I certainly would." Cindi and her husband are handsome, healthy, smart people, and yet she admits that it is constantly hard to affirm one another. What happens when there is so little to commend? How does love make a difference?
>
> Love is said to evaporate if the relationship is not mutual, if it's not physical, if the other person doesn't communicate, or if one party doesn't carry his or her share of the load. When I hear the litany of essentials for a happy marriage, I count off what my beloved can no longer contribute, and I contemplate how truly mysterious love is ("Muriel's Blessing." *Christianity Today*, Feb. 1996, p. 33).

Putting Principles into Practice

Put love into practice. We all know that knowing is one thing, but doing is something else. Here are a few tips for getting and keeping the love commitment strong and growing in your marriage:

For Both of You:

Learn each other's love languages. Husbands, ask your wife what ways she needs for you to best communicate your love to her. Wives, do the same with his love needs. Make a list of specifics and write them down. These can become your goals to work on in your relationship.

Husbands:

Get out your New Testament and read over the passage on love in Ephesians 5. If you really want to get radical, memorize the passage to let the reality of the picture of Christ and His church sink in. Then, be vulnerable with your wife. Ask her ways that you do get your love across. Also ask her what you are not doing that you should to encourage her with language to which she relates. Make it a habit to consistently love your wife in the ways she would like to be loved—her love language, not yours.

Wives:

In a gentle spirit and without nagging, try to help your husband understand your needs for love. Beyond the needs, help him learn the things he has done well in your marriage to communicate his love for you. Then share with him at the right moments, when he is open, ways that he can express his love in even better ways.

Both of You:

If you have been married for more than five years and you find yourself thinking that there is no love in your marriage, seek professional help. Before you give up, seek help from a solid Christian counselor or pastor who can guide you toward rebuilding your love.

Chapter 2

Decipher Her Differences

A Lifelong Study of the Feminine Nature

Guys, think about it! All your life you've had friends who are men, and now you're spending your life living with a person of the other gender. Rule number one: You can't treat her like you treat the guys.

Again, as obvious as that might seem initially, it remains the crux of many a marital conflict. So the better you understand her femininity, men, the better husband you'll be.

But understand this—studying your wife and womanhood is a lifetime pursuit for the caring husband.

2 Decipher Her Differences
A Lifelong Study of the Feminine Nature

Like most men, I, (Hans) grew up with lots of friends who were guys like me. I did not have many "girl" friends as a young boy. Sure, that came later in the teen years. But when we're preteen, it is pretty much guys hanging out with guys and girls with girls. The boys do "boy things" like playing with toy guns and tough sports and building model cars . . . at least that was the way it used to be. Today sports are still important, but now you also have video games thrown into the mix. Girls on the other hand tend to do the "girl things" like dressing up, playing with dolls, crafts, sharing secrets, doing hair and make-up. Though girls play sports too, their play often involves the "kinder, gentler" side of the equation. (But soccer certainly seems to be leveling the playing field in terms of aggressiveness these days.)

Now that we have our own sons and a daughter, we see this reality in our own home daily. Our daughter, Cambria, often feels ganged up on and squeezed out of her comfort zone by the overbearing testosterone levels of three brothers and a dad. She is just wired differently from A to Z! As a parent you can't help but see that there is a big difference between what boys do and what girls do when together.

But one day it all changes—boys literally wake up to the fact that girls are not so bad to be around—about the same day that certain hormones start kicking in!

Here is where the challenge begins. We begin our social life hanging out with members of the same sex and learn to treat them a certain way. But when we try to treat the opposite sex the same way, we run into trouble. A young man will soon realize that there's a whole lot he is going to have to learn when it comes to a woman—at least if he is going to make any progress in a relationship with one.

Now let's fast-forward to adulthood. Couples get married, and quickly the big adjustment begins. Soon after the honeymoon is over, the man realizes that this person he is now living with is extremely different than his previous roommates.

> ## Top 10 Tip
>
> A young man will soon realize that there's a whole lot he is going to have to learn when it comes to a woman—at least if he is going to make any progress in a relationship with one.

During my years in college, I had roommates as I lived off campus in various apartments. We guys had certain ways of taking care of our lives and things, and there were rarely conflicts. Each of the guys, no matter how many lived in the place, did his own thing. We're talking total independence here, coming and going as one pleases. Checking in with roommates was really not an issue.

But getting married and living with a female roommate is the dawning of a whole new dimension of experience for most men. Even if you had a sister growing up, that doesn't qualify you for understanding life with a woman.

Is the Woman Weaker?

It was soon after we got married in 1975 that I realized I did not really know Donna as I thought I did. We fell madly in love that summer of 1974, and after a short courtship, were married a year later. Obviously it is one thing to date and spend a lot of time together, but another to begin the lifelong adventure of marriage—as in living together morning and night: jungle breath, messy hair, no makeup, and all the rest!

When you're on a date and have a disagreement, you can go home and cool off. Most people in the dating/courtship phase of their relationship go in and out of emotional intimacy. At times you feel very close, and at other times you feel like breaking up. In those down times you can back off of the relationship for a while and let things slowly work themselves out. Not so when you are both living in the same house. Among the many new challenges you face, you have to work things out in the here and now—there is no other place to go, no escape.

For a man, living with a woman is a lifelong challenge—to do it right and to have a growing and satisfying relationship. Peter made this quite clear in the New Testament when he said,

> *Husbands, in the same way be considerate as you live with your wives, and treat them with respect as the weaker partner and as heirs with you of the gracious gift of life, so that nothing will hinder your prayers (1 Peter 3:7).*

Or, look at these same words in another translation:

> *In the same way you married men should live considerately with [your wives], with an intelligent recognition [of the marriage relation], honoring the woman as [physically] the weaker, but [realizing that you] are joint heirs of the grace*

*[God's unmerited favor] of life, in order that your prayers
may not be hindered and cut off—otherwise you cannot
pray effectively. (From the Amplified New Testament, copyright 1954, 1958, Lockman Foundation)*

Before proceeding, we need to pause to take a look at a thorny
issue within this passage from Peter. Many women resent, or at
least don't particularly like, Peter's comment about their being
the "weaker partner." What did Peter mean here, and is this a
put-down of a woman's strengths?

As a matter of fact, I can think of many times in our twenty-five
years of marriage when Donna has been much stronger than I
have. Since confession is good for the soul, here is my list of
issues where I've often seen Donna's greater strength:

- in consistent prayer for the family and children;

- in caring for the needs and concerns of family/friends;

- in discipline with the children;

- in tolerance of physical pain and sickness in general;

- in the courage it takes to deliver four children;

- in coping with the physical problems of our children;

- in relationships—she shows more empathy, compassion,
  and ability to understand the needs of other people; and

- in conflict resolution—she has a better grasp of the hidden issues that have caused the conflict.

It is tragic that some ill-informed men and women have used
these 1 Peter 3 verses against women at times to put them down
or "in their place." If they would study the words carefully, a
wonderful clarification emerges.

Let's take one more look at the passage and take apart a few of the important words:

> *Husbands, in the same way be considerate as you live with your wives, and treat them with respect as the weaker partner and as heirs with you of the gracious gift of life, so that nothing will hinder your prayers (1 Peter 3:7).*

So what exactly did Peter mean with this "weaker partner" comment? There are several key words in this passage for us husbands to zero in on with a laser focus:

Be considerate: another way to say this would be "dwell with them according to knowledge," or "according to the knowledge you have," as in trying to understand her physically, spiritually, and emotionally. During the days when the New Testament was written, there were many faulty views of men and women and the marriage relationship—pagan views that were certainly below those of Scripture. Today we have the same issues in our modern culture—unbiblical views have influenced many sincere Christians. But if we are going to dwell with our wives "according to knowledge," we clearly must look at our marriage relationship from the view of Scripture and what God has to say about it in His Word.

Treat them with respect: On the one hand, the husband recognizes her weaker power physically as a woman; on the other hand, he should view her with full equality spiritually. While much of worldly culture has said otherwise in history, the Bible has clearly taught spiritual equality for millennia. God views a woman as man's equal in receiving all of the grace of God. So she certainly deserves the husband's honor and is worthy of utter respect as an equal partner in the marital relationship. Indeed, any honest and experienced husband can attest that his wife's point of view can be a very helpful complement to his point of view, bringing insights into many situations where he may have been blindsided (see Gen. 2:18-25).

Weaker partner: The word weaker is *asthenestero* in Greek, referring to physical weakness, not intellectual inferiority. In the ancient pagan world, women were viewed as tools to be used. Their status was lower, and they were made to look like slaves to the needs of men. Peter fights that view with his treatment of woman, acknowledging her feminine side—which does encompass some aspects of her physical strength—while maintaining all of her worth and dignity. The husband must recognize that her weakness is physical, not intellectual, moral, or even (perhaps especially) emotional. In this knowledge it is his duty to care for her and protect her from any physical danger or undue burdens.

Heirs with you: This statement should put to rest any accusations that woman is in any way inferior to man in her nature. That is why Peter makes this statement in the context of how husbands should treat their wives: we are fellow heirs, joint heirs of all the good things that God holds in store for His children. This statement is best understood with the backdrop of knowledge of the times when these words were written. Today, laws protect a wife's rights in the West; but in ancient days (and still in some parts of the world today) justice is not so evident for wives. A man would pass on his wealth and inheritance to his sons with no rights for the wife whatsoever. But heavenly inheritance is not distributed according to earthly custom—our wives are joint heirs of everything!

How She Differs from the Guys

Clue number one: Open your eyes! But let's get deeper than just outward looks. In our years of marriage I have seen how Donna differs from my male friends in many ways. Some are quite obvious—we all agree that it's absolutely great God made them the physical beings that they are! But some other God-created feminine attributes are not so obvious to the average man.

Let's explore some of the differences. This is just a small sampling to get you thinking, and we're sure you can come up with many of your own.

Men and their manners: Now, guys, admit that you have certain behaviors around the men, including the various sounds we emit, gestures we make, and actions we take around the guys, that are really not appropriate with our wives. This would also include how dads act around their sons when there are no females present—similar to what would happen when a woman enters the men's locker room.

Men's crudeness when displayed in strictly males' presence makes women feel belittled. It reduces their sense of your respect for the special relationship you should have apart from you and your male friends.

Those "little" comments: These are the sarcastic, cutting remarks meant to be a put-down. For some reason guys find this happily barbaric way of communication to be endearing to their same sex. For example, a guy will walk into a room, see his buddy with a strange tie, and ask, "Did your mother-in-law give you that for Christmas?" Or "Did you get that tie in high school?"

If I made a comment like that to Donna, I don't have to tell you the results. But sometimes we cross this threshold and treat our mates too much like we treat the men. Before opening your mouth, guys, try asking yourself whether what you are about to say will come across lovingly. Let love be the ruler by which you measure your words. Think first—then try speaking to her.

Feedback: One of the toughest questions Donna ever asks me is, "Which of these two should I wear?" We all know what that's called—a lose/lose question. No matter which one I choose, it probably isn't going to be the right answer. What she really wants is affirmation. Now guys, you can't script this kind of scenario. But sometimes this response has helped me: "They're both beautiful, and I'd really be happy with either one. Which one do you think you want to wear?" When Donna tells me the answer, then she really wants me to affirm her choice. The same would hold true for earrings and just about anything. So what do I do if she puts on something I genuinely don't like? The answer to that question is simple: Nothing! Enjoy whatever she puts on and affirm her choices whenever you can, because unlike the guys, you have been called to love your wives.

Constructive Criticism: Here's a great story about how not to give your wife feedback regarding her looks or her clothing. Two friends of ours (who must remain absolutely anonymous, even to the general region of the country in which they live), recently told us this hilarious story, which certainly wasn't hilarious at the time. If you figure out who they are, we're dead.

It seems as though the wife had put on some weight due to some physical problems and the medication she was taking. One day her husband, (we'll call him Sam), walked into the bedroom and remarked to his wife (whom we'll label Sara), "Are those panties comfortable?" It seemed obvious from his intonation and comment that he could tell she was having a hard time fitting into things. She said nothing at the time except perhaps a noncommittal grunt. But later she went into what she called a "silent rage."

As soon as Sam left, Sara took out her scissors and cut up every single pair of panties that she had and threw them into the trash—except, of course, the ones she was wearing. She went to

Neiman Marcus, the most expensive store she could find at the local mall, marched into the lingerie section, then asked to see the most expensive panties sold. Using the family charge card, she stocked up on the next larger size, top of the line silk panties! The next time Sam saw her in these beautiful new panties, he commented on how attractive they looked. "Thanks," she said with a hint of revenge, "they're new. I thought you'd like them. You'll get the bill soon!"

Need we draw any conclusions from this story? What you as a husband might think is an innocent little piece of "constructive criticism" can start World War III in your marriage. So guard your tongue carefully (and read through James 3 whenever the urge to ease that guard comes upon you).

Independence: Have you ever noticed that Paul rarely exhorted wives to love their husbands? It assumes a common reality: women have a great capacity to love with a loving instinct that causes love to come more naturally to them. For them to express love to their husband is usually a given. Focusing upon it would generally amount to belaboring a non-issue.

On the other hand, since women are especially relational beings, needing to see love expressed regularly, Paul was inspired to exhort us husbands to love our wives. For one thing, we men tend to be independent. Most of us can go it alone for long periods on autopilot without any significant need for affection. So we are the ones who need the rebuke to love; our wives don't. That is a bottom-line difference between how we behave with the guys—that is independently—and how we treat that special one who is our life companion.

Communication in general: The best illustration I, Hans, ever heard regarding the difference between what men *think* they communicate to their wives and what their wives actually receive came from Gary Smalley the first summer I went to Promise Keepers. Sixty-five thousand men were gathered together in the Hoosier Dome in Indianapolis for a power-packed weekend of male bonding. As Gary Smalley spoke, he asked each one of us to pull one hair out of our heads, hold it up high, drop it, and watch it fall to the ground in front of us. We all did it and were curious about what would happen next. He asked us if we heard the hair as it crunched to the ground. Of course we didn't hear a thing, even though 65,000 hairs fell to the ground at the same time. (And you think you have trouble in your shower drain!)

Then Dr. Smalley asked every one of us to take off one of our shoes and hold it high up in front of us. On the count of three he asked us all to drop our shoes at the same time. Well, it sounded like a huge clap of rolling thunder as 65,000 shoes dropped to the floor of the stadium at one time. His point was this: When we think we're sharing a bit of constructive criticism with our wives, we view it as a small little hair we're dropping on her by way of correction. But generally they take it as if we've just hit them over the head with a boot. The moral of the story is this: Men, if you must try to give your wife constructive criticism, remember the hair versus the boot analogy. Timing and tenderness are everything. Wait for those reachable, teachable moments, and don't consider it your calling in life to improve the state of your mate.

The Study of Woman's Needs —A Lifelong Pursuit

In learning to understand the differences of the woman I have chosen to spend my life with, I need to know her true needs.

There was a time when I thought that was a no-brainer—surely, any guy could figure that out. But I have learned that Donna is totally different from any male friends I have, or ever will have; and I cannot really understand her needs without some help from outside.

I want to meet her needs so that we can have a growing, nurturing relationship and marriage. Marriage can be the greatest relationship in life—if you learn to meet one another's needs.

One of the best books we have seen on meeting the needs of one another is, *His Needs, Her Needs* by Willard F. Harley, Jr. (Fleming H Revell Co.). This classic marriage book is one of those *must get* books on surviving and thriving in a marriage. If you don't have it, go to your nearest bookstore and get it!

Dr. Harley is a licensed clinical psychologist and director of a network of mental health clinics and chemical dependency programs in Minnesota. He has had over three decades experience as a marriage counselor and has counseled hundreds of marriages—many of them in deep trouble. Dr. Harley believes that marriages

His Needs, Her Needs
by Dr. Willard F. Harley, Jr.

The Five Needs of Woman	The Five Needs of Men
Affection	Sexual fulfillment
Conversation	Recreational companionship
Honesty and openness	An attractive spouse
Financial support	Domestic support
Family commitment	Admiration

can be happy for a lifetime. And he has worked hard at helping bad marriages become good marriages, as well as broken marriages become whole again. For those of you who might have experienced the trauma of having one of the two of you involved in an extramarital affair, we especially recommend his book to you.

After reading this amazing book, we decided to personalize it for our marriage. The first insight we gained from Dr. Harley is this:

Marriage conflict is created in one of two ways:
Couples fail to make each other happy, or
Couples make each other unhappy

In his book, subtitled by the way, "Building an Affair-Proof Marriage," Dr. Harley tells of the many couples that fall into trouble with extramarital affairs because of this issue of needs not being met. The good news is that even if that has been your experience, help is possible. Get his book and learn his valuable lessons. We'll share more of his insights in Chapter Three on building good communication skills.

Our purpose here is not to go into deep marital therapy—we're really not qualified. But we do want to share with you some hints that have helped us in this arena. Specifically, I, Hans, made a list some time ago of the things I can do to meet Donna's needs—to make her happy. Aside from that being the right and honorable thing for me to do for her as her faithful husband, it makes life a whole lot more enjoyable as I live with her!

Here is my list, which I keep in my Palm Pilot, based on Dr. Harley's five basic needs of my wife:

How to Meet the Needs of My Wife— Deposits into Donna's Love Bank

1 Affection: Her essential cement of the relationship.

Hugs

Flowers

Greeting cards

Holding hands

Back rubs (without sex)

The good-night and good-bye kiss

Call her during the day.

Leave hidden messages while away during travel.

2 Conversation: focused on Donna

Never ask, "About what?" if she asks to talk!

When I get home, try to get alone with her and find out how her day went.

Take her out for coffee or lunch.

Take a "talk walk" after work.

Pursue overlapping areas of mutual interest like camping.

Caring partners converse in a caring way.

She needs undivided attention breaks.

3 Honesty and openness

Truthfulness is the key—period.

4 Financial support

Provide for the family's needs.

5 Family commitment

I need to be a good and consistent father.

Plan to spend quality family time with the whole family, and make sure it is a pattern throughout their growing years.

Agree with Donna and engage with her in family standards, rewards, and punishments.

I'd like to add one more arena for those of you who travel a lot, like I do. When I get home from a business trip, there is a familiar pattern. I am tired and focused on two things: (1) what happened in the city where I was, and (2) getting back into the mountain of things that piled up for me while I was away.

To fight the battle of neglecting Donna and the kids when I return, I have developed some guidelines to help the reentry process. These are special rules that come into play when I return home. We develop a more complete travel guide for husbands in Chapter Six, but here is my short list for starters:

Reentry

Special Tips for Trip Returns:

- Always plan a special debriefing time with Donna over a lunch or coffee away from home. Ask her questions and listen to her answers. Focus first on what happened to *her* while I was gone.
- Take some time off from work to catch up with my chores around the house.
- Give her time to warm up to my being involved again in the daily routine.
- Take the kids off her back for a few hours.

Finally, here's my "Top Five," my short list of things I try to remember to do more than anything else to meet her needs. If I have just a little bit of energy or time for expressing love, I know these are the top proven methods to fill her love bank:

Summary Top List of Meeting Donna's Needs: "The Tried and True Top Five"

1 Sit and listen to her day.

2 Bring her flowers.

3 Send or leave her cards.

4 Take the kids off her hands.

5 Do the dishes. This covers a multitude of sins!

Hero Husbands We Know

Scott is a hero husband of grand proportions. His wife is not well, and he has learned through years of struggle what it means to love his wife and care for her as a "tender" vessel needing nurturing and special care.

Recently, I (Hans) had the opportunity to attend a special summit meeting on the east coast for CEOs who are in similar types of work to mine. Scott was there, but not for long. This once-a-year summit, a small intimate gathering of high-potency influencers, is always something that I look forward to. It's a chance to rub shoulders with men in positions similar to mine, and a great opportunity to receive encouragement. So much of my life involves giving to others, and this is one of the few times of the year that I am on the receiving end and able to receive encouragement from others who understand the unique challenges of my position. I go for male bonding and to get my needs met from other men.

We all arrived at the retreat center in Pennsylvania on a cold evening in February. In fact, Scott and I flew in on the same plane from Chicago. At the airport he called his wife and discovered that she was not doing well with an ongoing illness she struggles with. Later that night, after we had concluded our evening session, he called his wife again to learn that she was not doing well at all. In the morning after breakfast we each shared our personal prayer requests around the breakfast table.

When Scott concluded his sharing, he told us that he needed to take off and go back home to care for his wife. It was not that she was in any critical danger, but she was feeling very much alone and had a sense of helplessness without her husband by her side. We took time out to pray for him and his wife, and

"A Little Glance Goes a Long Way" Just Let Her Know You Care

from Ruth Ryan

Ruth Ryan, wife of legendary pitcher Nolan Ryan, recalls the one moment that stands out for her in Ryan's illustrious 26-year career:

"It probably happened the first time on the baseball diamond in Alvin, Texas, in the mid-1960s. Then it happened repeatedly for three decades after that. Inevitably, sometime during a game, Nolan would pop up out of the dugout and scan the stands behind home plate, looking for me. He would find my face and grin at me, maybe snapping his head up in a quick nod as if to say, 'There you are; I am glad.' I'd wave and flash him a smile. Then he would duck under the roof and turn back to the game. It was a simple moment, never noted in record books or career summaries. But of all the moments in all the games, it was the one most important to me."

(From Ruth Ryan's book, *Covering Home,* Word Books, as quoted on page 87 of *Readers Digest*, Sept. 1995.)

sent him on his way with concern for their well being. He had come all this way to one of the most important weekends in his calendar year, only to turn right around to go back home. Scott did that to stand next to his lifetime partner, "be there" for his wife. The nineteen of us who remained at the meeting agreed unanimously that Scott is a hero husband for doing the right thing in a moment like this. She needed his support and his protection in the face of uncertainty, and Scott chose to lay aside his own needs to meet hers. Sounds a lot to us like Christ loving the church in the way He gave Himself for her.

Putting Principles into Practice

If you're convinced that your wife is not really just like the other people in your life, then try to sort out some of the ways that she differs. Specifically:

For Both of You:

Read 1 Peter 3:7 together and discuss its meaning. What do these words mean to you in your marriage? Look up the passage in several commentaries and write down the explanations that you find. Then read the passage in several other translations of the Bible.

Husbands:

How would you apply 1 Peter 3:7 in your marriage? Take some time to write some notes in your journal about how you should use the truths in this passage as you relate to your wife.

Go through our list of annoying things that husbands do to turn off their wives in this chapter under the heading, "How

She Differs from the Guys." Do you find any habits here that you are guilty of? Try discussing them with your wife and see how she feels. Better yet, work at being more of a gentleman in private and see what difference it makes.

Both of You Together:

Go away for a weekend, or at least overnight, to a nice hotel where you can relax for a quiet evening. Then on the next morning take a couple of hours to discuss the five needs of a wife from Dr. Harley's list. If you are committed to understanding your spouse and meeting her needs, ask her to help you make your personal application list.

Wives:

Do not hold any list that your husband makes in good faith over his head as a tool against him. Give him grace and encourage him when he hits a home run. Remember this is a process that can take many months and years to develop.

Chapter 3

Speak No Evil

Communication and Conflict Strategies

Be careful with your words—they cannot be re-thrown like a bad pitch. The man who is used to waging heated arguments in the marketplace thinks little of the emotional fallout when it is over. He can have a strong argument with a colleague or friend and forget about it an hour later as they go on their merry ways. Not so in a marriage—if you've been married for any period of time, you have most likely found that the way you say what you say can do more damage than the content of your words.

For instance, a woman often needs responding more than reasoning when her needs are not being met. So avoid the "I've got to fix her problem" attitude.

Husbands and wives need to look under the surface when tempers flare, find the source of frustration, and deal with the issues at that level.

Speak No Evil
Communication and Conflict Strategies

The night before I was to leave on a long overseas trip to Asia, Donna and I planned a romantic evening. We got the kids to bed early in order to have lots of time to communicate in all the right ways, if you get the drift.

What ensued was the opposite of what we wanted most—because of the strange mood I found myself in. I admit it; *it was entirely my fault.* I, Hans, began a downward spiraling argument about some great concern that I can't even remember anymore.

In fact, tonight as I write these words, I asked Donna if she could remember what the argument was about. We both remember that it was one of the most hurtful disagreements we've had in years. And yet the amazing thing is, as we sit here tonight and try to remember what it was about, we can't. I thought it would be a great illustration to use here, but then I said to Donna, "Wait a minute. Let's not bring it up because it has obviously been buried." Really—the truth—I was worried that we would remember what it was about and start it all over again. But that was not going to be a problem.

Donna improved on my thought when she said, "No, it hasn't been buried; it's been forgiven and forgotten." That was the beauty of what happened that night: We *did* resolve it before we went to sleep. We did not let the sun go down on our anger (Eph.. 4:26). We didn't want to go to sleep with it unresolved, nor could I have taken off for the airport without our hearts being right with one another. We worked through our misunderstanding . . . even enjoyed physical intimacy before dozing off to sleep. Talk about the full range of emotions all in one evening!

Exploring the Depths of Disagreements

When I was a young boy, I loved cave exploring. One of the things that I often did with my Boy Scout troop was to go on camp-outs in northern Alabama near forests that were filled with caves to explore. Since these were unprotected caves with no guides, we had to be careful that we left a trail along the way as we explored deep into these dark caverns. In fact, we would usually take some sort of marking system or even string so we could retrace our steps when necessary.

Arguments are very much like exploring caves. Once you have fallen into the depths of a disagreement or conflict with your spouse, there are two options:

1 *Dig yourself in deeper*—accelerate the hurtfulness and dig the wounds deeper, causing more distancing (which is equivalent to getting *lost* in the cave, a *real* dead end!);

Or

2 *Backtrack*—find your way out and try to find your way back to the opening that led into this cave (back to the origin, shedding "light" to search out the real causes/issues).

Clearly, number 2 is the right choice: begin the healing process by going back to the beginning of the feelings that led to the hurtfulness. Just recently, while I was balancing the checkbook, I lashed out at Donna for writing so many checks. She keeps a

From Robertson McQuilken,
quoting his wife Muriel

"Once, before we signed off for sleep, I was winning the argument with irresistible logic when she raised up on one elbow, transfixed me with fire in her grey-green eyes, and said, 'Well, let me tell you something. Logic's not everything, and feeling's not nothing.'"

From Muriel's Blessing, *Christianity Today (Feb. 5, 1996) p. 34.*

record of the checks that she writes in her check ledger (quite faithfully, I might add), and then I transcribe that information to my computer. I lashed out at her and hurt her deeply that night. The feelings just escalated because she naturally felt defensive about what I was accusing her of.

As we chilled out and calmed down, I realized it was not her spending that caused my frustration, but it was the pressure I felt to balance the family budget when there are so many expenses related to running a large household. I channeled my general, personal frustration about the lack of enough money at her. In fact, I've often seen that when I attack her for no apparent reason, and we sit back and analyze what is going on, it becomes obvious that she is the one closest to me and whom happens to be most convenient and "safe" to unload my frustration upon. The frustration is going to fly; she just happens to be the closest target.

We have met some people who are proud to say they never fight. Perhaps you're thinking, "Why, Hans and Donna, all this talk about arguing is totally foreign to us. We have such a great maturity and understanding in our marriage that we never argue."

Recently a couple told us that their parents are very proud that they have never fought in their whole married lives. This couple said to us, "You know why they don't fight? Because they have a declared, permanent, ice-cold truce." There is no way a male and a female living together can keep from having some sort of disagreements from time to time. If you're not comfortable calling them arguments, then you probably wouldn't ever use the terminology "fight." Then you might just want to leave it at the concept of "disagreement"—okay, that's a word we can all agree on.

What's the Real Issue Here?

"For women, talk is the ultimate intimacy," says Deborah Tannen, internationally acclaimed expert on communication, in her new book, *I Only Say This Because I Love You.* "But men don't feel that way at all," she observes. We guys are usually uncomfortable talking about our feelings. According to Tannen's research, men talk like report cards ("How was my day? B+"). Men create friendships by doing things together; women create their bonds by telling secrets and getting very personal about all aspects of their lives. Tannen says that women's "rapport" talk verses men's "report" talk promotes much of the miscommunication that creates the arguments.

> **Top 10 Tip**
>
> **Swapping Pet Peeves**
>
> From a creative negotiating wife:
>
> "If you both have annoying habits—and who doesn't—try offering up one of yours for one of his: 'I'll try to leave the mail in one place so you can find it if you'll try not to leave your dirty socks on the floor of the closet.' "

Let's go back to the major conflict that flared up between the two of us over that hubcap, lost in a blowout. Our conflict arose over our total opposite perspectives on the same event.

Since Donna appears "fine" to Hans (a B+ or better!), he could not get why she didn't use the time to look for the lost hubcap. But to Donna the whole incident is of major proportion in its seriousness. She wants to debrief about the trauma she had experienced.

Just to recall the facts, Hans had gone out of town to Pennsylvania to speak at a weekend conference. Donna was on her way back home with the van, after speaking at a women's conference in Iowa. As she drove home, she had a blowout on a dark and secluded road in the middle of nowhere in northern Illinois. Fortunately she did manage to get help, and after quite an ordeal made it home safely around midnight.

When Hans returns home and happens to look in the garage, he notices that the hubcap is missing on the van. He has no clue of the storm that will erupt by uttering these four words: *"Where is the hubcap?"* Donna becomes very angry and hurt that Hans would even think to question her about the location of a "stupid hubcap," considering all she has gone through alone.

Hans, on the other hand, merely wants to know if she has looked around for the hubcap while she sat on the side of the road for an hour waiting for a tow truck. "Look around for the hubcap?" she retorts with a rising fury. "You think I'm going to get out of the car in the middle of nowhere in the rain on a dark, empty highway with *no* flashlight in my dress clothes and backtrack along the road to look for a stupid lost hubcap!" The reality and powerful *emotion of Donna's trauma* is having a head-on collision with the *logic of Hans' sense of responsibility* to care for the automobile.

As a further backdrop, and to better understand my (Hans') reasoning, I had recently replaced another stolen hubcap on her van at a cost of $85. I didn't want to think about the cost of another new hubcap on top of the cost of a new tire, and having the automobile towed home! To put it mildly, this was a true blue, state of the art, bona fide, major argument between two people who think they understand each other after twenty years of negotiating a warm and healthy relationship.

Let's take apart the pieces of this argument and try to understand what was going on. Why was Donna so upset at my question about the hubcap? And why was I so upset about losing the hubcap? For Donna, she had been through the dangerous trauma, as a woman alone, in a state of exhaustion, in the dark, along a lonely highway in the middle of nowhere. What she needed from me was tenderness, care, concern, and empathy for the horrible experience she had gone through. *My question communicated to her that I didn't care about what had happened to her, but rather that I cared only about the car.* To her thinking, I was communicating that the *car* was of greater value than the *wife.*

Of course, in my way of thinking, nothing could be further from the truth. She was obviously home safe and sound, so everything was fine. The immediate problem was that the hubcap was gone. Therefore it seemed to me that Donna was fixed, but the car was broken. No matter how logically I might have approached the situation, I put a serious breach in the relationship by lacking sensitivity to her needs. I could have escalated the situation and made it even worse by pressing her as to why she didn't look around for the hubcap. It certainly was going through my mind, but fortunately I had enough sense to shut up.

One major thing I *should* have done to show my true love and concern for her (but didn't) was—simply express my joy at her safe return by taking her in my arms and saying, "Wow, I am so glad you weren't injured or worse, honey. I don't know what I would have done if you had been hurt!" By the way, I didn't figure this out on my own. She had to coach me all the way.

Avoid the "A" and "N" Words

It happened again the other night. You would think after all these years we would learn how inflammatory the "a" and "n" words are. Donna said to me, "You *always* leave the dirty dishes in the sink for me." I can assure you that comment raised my blood temperature immediately. Want to guarantee an all-out war of words with your spouse? Try these two bombshell words as you assassinate the character of the other: "You *always* . . ." and "You *never* . . ."

Now I have to admit that I am just as guilty as she is. On a recent occasion when we were late for an important engagement—and of course I, Hans, was cooling my heels at the back door waiting for her—I concluded it was Donna's fault. I could not resist letting the words flow out of my mouth even though I knew they wouldn't be well received, "We *never* make it anywhere on time." Of course, I was implying that it was because of her that we never make it anywhere on time, and thus I was saying directly to her, "You are *always* making us late." It was not a pretty sight.

When we try to take apart the dynamics of a situation like that, we realize that neither one of us is telling the truth. There is never a time in a marriage when a situation merits using the words "always" or "never." And yet we like to say those things because of anger that tends to boil up inside of us out of frustration. What we have tried to do as a couple is covenant with each other that we will avoid whenever possible—meaning we'll try to *never* use it—the "a" and "n" words of "always" and "never." Why are these words so destructive? Because they tend to write off a person in one, quick, heartless judgment. It gives the recipient no hope for improvement and a helpless feeling that it's an area in which that they are complete failures. And since the recipient usually doesn't agree with this statement, it's the perfect setup for a heated conflict.

What would be the right thing to do in a situation like this? The right thing for me would have been to say, "Donna, I am feeling very frustrated about being late to this important engagement. Is there anything we could do to try to avoid this happening again?" And for her, instead of heaping guilt upon me for "never" doing the dishes in the evening, she should say something like, "Hans, I need for you to do the dishes more often. Carrying the load together makes a real difference to me. It's very discouraging to me to wake up with a sink full of dirty dishes in the morning."

Top **10** *Tip*

Want to guarantee an all-out war of words with your spouse? Try these two bombshell words as you assassinate the character of the other:

"You *always* . . ."

or

"You *never* . . ."

The bottom line is this: avoid the words that are going to be inflammatory. Instead, try to share with one another how you are feeling, and in a loving and gentle way try to indicate what specific change your spouse could make to improve the situation. It's not the natural approach that any of us take because of our own selfish natures, but it is the high road of maturity, which will make for a much stronger relationship.

Why Tempers Flare

In our experience and study, we've learned that any couple who never argues or disagrees in their relationship is usually in deep denial. Hopefully, as a couple matures and adjusts to one another, the frequency of conflicts will lessen through the years of marriage. But the reality is that when two people live so closely together and deal with the pressures of life, they will have conflicting viewpoints and attitudes from time to time.

We have isolated the most *common* reasons for the escalation of conflict between husband and wife:

> **Needs not being met**—If conflict arises over something that seems insignificant or trite, before allowing tensions to escalate, *look deeper!* Ask, "Is there something I have done to offend (or hurt) you?" If not, ask, "Are you feeling pressure from something that I could help relieve?" Usually you will discover a deeper issue that needs attention. (Remember backtracking out of the cave into the "light" of origin?)

> **Differing expectations**—Communication is the key to preventing conflict. Stop before reacting, communicate "where you are coming from," and ask your spouse to share his or her perspective or outlook. Taking the time to share your expectations regarding a given decision or problem and making the effort to understand one another will often resolve the issue. The radical differences in perspective may not easily be understood, but we *must* come to accept one another as part of mutual submission in love (Eph.. 5:21—"Submit to one another out of reverence for Christ").

Displaced anger—Stress often can come from outside sources, such as overwork, demands and needs of children, financial concerns, or fatigue. Any of these can be cause for you to lash out upon your spouse—the safe one to "vent" on. Stop! Remember, angry words will only escalate the situation. Tell your partner what it is you are really dealing with, and allow him or her to "bear your burden" with you! Who better to do this than your mate? "Carry each other's burdens, and in this way you will fulfill the law of Christ" (Gal. 6:2). The "law of Christ" is, of course, to *love* one another! (James 2:8)

Violation of rights—Mutual respect for one another is the bottom line here. *Assume* little! Each of you must have the perspective of your spouse. Make a practice of talking through together *all* decisions that affect the family. This should be an inviolable rule. It relieves pressure on either partner when it becomes necessary to decide something alone.

Personality conflicts—Find ways to meet each other halfway when your basic tendencies cause conflict. Both must give—don't expect your mate to be the only one to change. For example, I, Donna, have adjusted as a *very* open "people person" to Hans' more private ways by not "bearing all" to everyone. I am more selective with whom I share our family and personal information. Hans, on the other hand, has adjusted his naturally hard-nosed Germanness to be more tender and expressive, to show loving concern if I'm stressed out or tired.

Dramatically different family backgrounds—Hans' studies in corporate culture were very helpful to us in this area. Although we had already adjusted to one another's differences in many ways, we didn't truly understand the *impact* of family culture until we had been married fourteen years! We have a true cross-cultural marriage with Hans having been raised in a strong German subculture in Alabama, while I was raised in a very American and emotionally open Christian home. My family expressed love constantly and openly, whereas these German folk in their culture would not openly express their love or personal feelings.

We strongly believe that this area of family culture gives us our most basic instincts. As no two families are alike, *every* marriage *will* have culture conflicts that must be worked through. "My way is the right way" is a natural way to feel, but it takes maturity on the part of both in a marriage to adapt and give up some of those ways that offend or conflict with your spouse. Our favorite professor at Columbia International University, Mr. Buck Hatch, used to call some of those ways "Tremendous Trifles"—such as the particular way we squeeze the toothpaste. He confirmed that they are only the tip of the iceberg that lies below—that basic culture and way of looking at life that each of us has.

Every man and woman is unique. We believe that by "becoming one flesh" and "leaving and cleaving," through marriage, God can help us study, accept, adapt, learn from, and even love those differences in each other. But it takes commitment and work, and it must be looked at as a mutual journey of discovery.

Hero Husbands We Know

This story is not really about healing conflicts, but more about being insensitive, which is a root cause of disagreements and unhappiness in marriage. Ron and Jamie have been married for seven years. For six of those seven, Ron did nothing for Valentines Day. Maybe he figured that he got his valentine and married her. Thus, there was no need anymore to make a big deal with red hearts and roses. Wrong!

How does Jamie feel when Ron does nothing? She feels unappreciated and unloved as well. Many women feel a sense of being taken for granted by their husbands when they act (or fail to act) this way. She starts to feel like the TV or the furniture or refrigerator—just another one of the conveniences in his life, ready and waiting when he needs it.

Finally, after six years of neglect, Jamie got through to Ron. He came to understand that it really made her feel unloved and unnoticed when he did nothing on Valentine's Day. I'm not sure if it was a sledgehammer or a crowbar, but the message finally got through.

I think what Ron did deserves our hero husband award for Valentine's Day. First, he took the day off from work. Second, he asked her to go shopping at the places of her choice—including going through lots of those little feminine stores with knickknacks and fancy frills. Ron would have preferred the hardware department at Sears, but he hung tough and spent several hours with her going through the shops.

But that's not all! Ron called one of Jamie's best friends a few days early to do some research. This guy really went all out! He discovered that Jamie was tired of her hair the way it was and wished so much for the chance to try something totally new— a complete makeover. But since she knew it was out of the question with their budget, she didn't even mention it. Well, after the shopping time in the early afternoon, Ron surprised Jamie and took her to a fancy hair styling salon downtown for a complete makeover. What a hit! Home run with Jamie? Absolutely.

He filled her love bank and communicated in loud tones that he loves her and the role she plays in their marriage.

One postscript on this story: a smart thing Ron did was call a good friend of Jamie's and ask for advice about how to communicate that he really loves her. We have seen men do things that they think will make their wives happy, only to bomb out and make matters worse. Don't be too proud, men—ask an expert: a woman.

Putting Principles into Practice

Arguments in a marriage can at times be a really good thing, according to expert Deborah Tannen, whom we mentioned earlier in this chapter. After years of observing couples communicate, she concludes, "Sometimes fighting is healthy if it forces people to confront issues that they would otherwise sweep under the rug." So she has four rules for fighting:

1 Be careful how you give suggestions or criticisms—be sure you don't do more harm that good.

2 Fight fairly—stick to the topic and avoid pulling up the past. Try to stay constructive.

3 Discuss fighting when you aren't fighting—discuss what you should try not doing when you do fight.

4 Use humor—find ways to relieve the tension of a fight with humor.

We have come up with these guidelines as we have worked through communication strategies in our own marriage. The best way to work out an argument is to take the following steps:

- Stop the hurtful words.

- Never use "always" or "never."

- Cool off.

- Reflect on your feelings.

- Ask what's down deeper.

- Don't let the sun go down on your anger.

- Forgive and forget.

- Seek help if necessary.

If you have a pattern of consistent arguments and conflicts in your marriage, you should probably seek professional help from a pastor or counselor. We would also encourage you as a first step to look at our list of "Why Tempers Flare" earlier in this chapter. Try to identify what causes conflict in your marriage. Perhaps you can find the right teachable moments to discuss the list together.

A few final thoughts on finding a "Win/Win" situation in marriage. Make *praise* a practice in your marriage! It is so much easier to see the problems and weaknesses in our mates, and it's common to let stress overcome us and just simply react to our circumstances. That's where conflict gets to be habit—an easy, lazy reaction. Make it your practice to praise your wife. Look for the good things in

> ### Wisdom from Solomon
>
> "Starting a quarrel is like breaching a dam;
> so drop the matter before a dispute breaks out."
> —*Proverbs 17:14*

her. Gary Smalley reminds us of the great power of praise: "I can vividly remember my boss saying years ago, 'If only I had ten men like you, we could change the world.' After that, I was so motivated I couldn't do enough for him."

Teachers know how praise motivates children. One teacher said she praised each student in her third-grade class every day, without exception. Her students were the most motivated, encouraged, and enthusiastic in the school. When my (Hans') high school geometry teacher praised me regularly, my "D" average climbed to an "A" in six weeks.

Conflict often arises because couples focus on the negative. Praise flows out of gratitude for what you DO have, not dwelling on what you DON'T have. Knowing how significant praise can be, why do we as husbands fail to express it to our wives? The most common reason is preoccupation with our own needs, vocation, and activities. We lose sight of the positive and helpful qualities in our wives when we are preoccupied. Even worse, we fail to acknowledge our wives' helpful traits when we do notice them.

When a husband forgets his wife's need for praise, the marriage is usually on its way downhill. So how can we grow in this area of encouragement and praise toward our wives? When you think about your wife, dwell on those things in her that are true, noble, right, pure, lovely, admirable, excellent, and praise-worthy (Phil. 4:8). Certainly the "excellent wife" in Proverbs 31 was very "together" and successful largely because her husband believed in her, and his love overflowed in praise! "Her children arise and call her blessed; her husband also, *and he praises her:* Many women do noble things, but you surpass them all" (Prov. 31:28-29, italics added). *Wow!* Any woman would respond positively to that kind of statement!

Chapter

4

Find Her Frequency

Sharpen Your Listening Skills

Men think vertically. Men want women to get on with their lives, so that they can go back to watching 'Combat' reruns."—Tim Allen

Something about tears always seems to get a man's attention.

She doesn't want me to give her a quick, five-minute solution with ten easy steps to put this problem behind her. She needs me to listen to her, to know I care, to feel her hurt, and to sense her pain. Being a bottom-line, let's-fix-the-problem kind of guy, just sitting and listening is a big stretch for me.

Be that as it may, there is still no substitute for quiet, prolonged exposure of one soul to another.

Find Her Frequency
Sharpen Your Listening Skills

Acouple of summers ago we were tooling down the freeways of Wyoming, enjoying a blissful family vacation getaway. The four children were happily playing in the back as Donna sat next to me in the copilot's chair of our family motor home. The only thing wrong with the picture that day was that my radar antenna was shut down.

Family vacations are always a great time for the Finzels. Donna especially looks forward to the hours that we will have alone, sitting in the pilot and copilot seats of our traveling home-away-from-home. For her, it is a time to really debrief on a deeper level about everything that has been going on in both of our lives since the last time we went camping.

Unfortunately, as is the case for most of the men I know, I just seem to want to sit quietly and vegetate when I am driving down the freeway. In fact, I'm amazed at how many other couples have this same experience. The woman just can't understand why the man doesn't want to talk when they're finally alone. The man, on the other hand, finds his relaxation by just driving down the road endlessly, hour after hour, with only an occasional grunt of "yes" or "no."

I (Hans) personally find that one of the most relaxing things I can do is to just drive and be alone with my thoughts. Of course, I admit that I am not an avid conversationalist like some of my male friends. I'm sure there are some husbands who love to chatter as they tool down the freeways, but more often than not there is a communications challenge. You would think that when a husband and wife are finally together with uninterrupted hours before them, the words would just begin to flow. But that's really not the case. One of the great challenges is to break through the comfortable clog—clear the sludge out of the pipes, and get the words flowing between husband and wife.

On this particular day, as we were enjoying the breathtaking beauty of Wyoming's open range, stretching out endlessly toward the horizon, Donna was becoming more and more exasperated by my disinterest in communication. I think if she had access to a large 2x4, she probably would have whacked me on the head to get my attention. Finally, she broke into tears, which . . . yes, you know it too . . . is much more effective than a 2x4! Women's tears do that to men.

> ## Summer Vacations
>
> One of the great challenges of a vacation is to break through the comfortable clogs, clear the sludge out of the pipes, and get the words flowing between husband and wife.

What is it about tears that always seem to get a man's attention? As soon as I saw the tears begin to flow, I said to myself, "Oh! I guess this is really serious stuff to her." I am amazed at how hard-hearted I can be sometimes, but I'll readily tune out her needs. Donna began to pour out her heart to me about how difficult the last months had been—I was gone so much in my travels, and she was left home alone to fend for herself with all the responsibilities of the home and the four children.

"I've reached the limit, the edge . . . I mean it," she cried. "Something's got to give. I don't know what's over that edge, but I *know* it's not good! I just can't go on with our life this way." What followed was a long conversation about the cumulative effect on her of bearing the weight of our home life as I traveled. We dug into her needs and my role in helping to take care of them. We discussed options and mostly I just listened to her talk. A man's response is always to try to fix the problem, but for once I bit my lip, kept my mouth shut, and tried to listen intensely as she poured out her heart to me.

I'm finally learning that the process of *pouring out her heart* is extremely important to Donna. She doesn't want me to give her a quick, five-minute solution with ten easy steps to put this problem behind us. She needs me to listen to her, to know I care, to feel her hurt, and to sense her pain. Being a bottom-line, let's-fix-the-problem kind of guy, just sitting and listening is a big stretch for me.

That talk was one where she finally got through to me—it was the beginning of a healing time for us. In the subsequent months I began to take concrete steps to change my schedule and my approach to traveling, since I finally realized the unusual pressure it placed on her. I consider Donna a super-woman, but constantly expecting superhuman efforts on her part was at the very least unfair. Our hearts go out to the many single parents who literally do have to be everything to the children they raise while

Top **10** *Tip*

Just Shut Up And Listen

"A man's response is always to try to fix the problem, but I bit my lip, kept my mouth shut, and tried to listen intensely as she poured out her heart to me."

they are trying to bring home a paycheck and make ends meet. And the reality is, they too need support, from family, community, and the church (but that's another subject for another book).

On Listening and Other Rare, Exotic Habits

Any of us who are task-oriented, type A, obsessive-compulsive males especially must learn to slow down and let people into our lives. It may be popular in our hectic paced culture to be a fast-tracker with a full day timer, but we will impact people spiritually and permanently only by careful, deliberate, one-on-one contact. In this age of telecommunications and voice messaging, *there is still no substitute for quiet, prolonged exposure of one soul to another.* With all the marvels of the Internet and a reach-out-and-touch-someone technology, husband and wife are more in need of quiet and prolonged communication than ever before. The more busy and crazy our lives become, the more communication protects the marriage.

As Donna indicated previously, I am a full-blooded German. I also tend to be *task-oriented* by nature. Since I find myself in roles of leadership, I often think about how my Germanness affects my leadership relationships. It is an unfair generalization to say that Germans are all task-oriented. So I'll just leave it as a matter-of-fact statement that many of the Germans I know tend to be perfectionistic workaholics who rarely relax, and they tend to foster rather rigid relationships. Sure, there are exceptions, but not among the many Germans I've known!

So my beautiful, relationally oriented wife is always calling out to me, *"Hans, stop! Can't you just sit down for an hour and do nothing? Could we just talk?"* That is extremely hard for me . . . especially the doing-nothing part. I guess deep down in my

74

task-oriented nature, I see talking as not really accomplishing all that much. I tend to be an impatient conversationalist . . . that is, unless I am in a deep discussion that is driving me toward the accomplishment of another task, or unless I am in a situation where I cannot get to my work and have some downtime. Even when we go camping, I tend to spend my time tinkering with the equipment instead of just vegetating (which I've been told is the goal of this camping business). Now I have made good progress in recent years, and I am learning to slow down, mostly due to Donna's persistent influence.

When I talk to other men about this common ailment of obsessive behavior, they all seem to have the same problem—that is, their wives don't feel like they take enough time to listen. Tim Allen of "Home Improvement" fame summarizes it well:

> Men don't listen, particularly to women. This shouldn't be a big surprise. A woman will talk and talk and talk about some problem until a man cuts her off and says, "Here's what I'd do." Men are always giving advice out of their own experience. Men think vertically. Some guy is always bigger, badder, better. His car is nicer, his job more lucrative, his women prettier. Men live to vanquish those challenges. They don't mind helping a woman overcome her problems, if only she'll listen. Men want women to get on with their lives, so that they can go back to watching "Combat" reruns (*Don't Stand Too Close to a Naked Man,* Tim Allen, p. 210).

Well . . . I (Donna) am going to share a news flash with all you men out there who care to listen up. *Women don't want to hear your advice!* They don't want solutions to their crises. They just want an arm around their shoulders and a soft-spoken,

"I understand" (if you do!) or "I hear you, and I care about how you're feeling" (if you don't!).

Women want to:

- **see** that you care about their interests;
- **feel** your closeness and love; and
- **know** you have truly heard them.

Just to make sure it is getting through to you, I'm going to say it one more time:

Guys, women don't want to hear your advice!

In Chapter Two we briefly mentioned 1 Peter 3, where Peter spoke of the responsibilities of husbands and wives. So many times the subject of submission is the focus of teaching from this passage. As I (Donna) studied this passage for teaching last year, I was amazed to learn new meaning in these verses. Verse 7 reads, *Husbands, in the same way be considerate as you live with your wives, and treat them with respect as the weaker partner and as heirs with you of the gracious gift of life, so that nothing will hinder your prayers.* The words normally translated "weaker vessel" or "weaker partner" can also be translated literally, "feminine one." Our uniqueness as women is clear in this passage. Peter knew that, and he wrote clearly that God commands husbands to:

- **be considerate living with your wife,**
- **treat her with respect,**
- **understand her unique feminine needs, and**
- **remember she is your coheir of salvation.**

If husbands fail to do those things, Peter said that their prayers would be hindered. That's powerful! Here we see again the foundation of all we want to convey in this book. If husbands will truly love their wives in this way, we believe their marriages and home life will be revolutionized.

At the top of the list of "feminine ways" is the woman's basic need for *affection*. In response to our nonscientific survey of married couples, this issue came through both as the number one need of women, and as the one most husbands fail to meet in their wives. Let's repeat that here, since we're talking about communication skills and a husband's need to listen to the needs of his wife: at the top of the list of "feminine ways" is the woman's basic need for **affection.**

Top **10** On Effective Communication Skills *Tip*

From a newly arrived "empty nester" couple in Iowa:

"We value effective communication highly in our marriage. The empty nest is a good revealer of the communication skills we have—good or bad.

"We have found our marriage to be like a bank: investments in communication have paid off over time. If we frequently deposit the 1 Corinthians 13 type of love—forgiveness, companionship, commitment, and spiritual respect—there will be greater rewards from which to draw in later years."

In his book, *Learning to Live with the One You Love,* Jim Smith reveals that women have a desperate need for closeness—to be connected in their relationship with their husbands. Men, to the contrary, fear closeness and actually feel safer with distance. Obviously, this creates barriers to affection (closeness) in husbands. Ironically, one of a man's greatest needs—sexual satisfaction—won't usually be responded to by his wife unless she first *feels close* to him!

Listening Carefully to Her Intimate Needs

We hesitated to write this book because of the flood of books already on the market in the area of Christian marriage. Who needs another book on marriage anyway? However, we were finally convinced to write the book by taking this unique approach of looking at, most specifically, how the husband can do a better job of living his role and fulfilling his responsibilities. Men, if you're reading this, at the top of your list of responsibilities must be *"Find her frequency."*

As we briefly mentioned in Chapter Two, of all the books we have read on marriage, without a doubt our number one favorite is *His Needs, Her Needs: Building an Affair-Proof Marriage,* by Dr. Willard F. Harley, Jr. Nothing has helped us more in our own marriage. Willard Harley's underlying philosophy of a good marriage is simple and profound:

> *"Become aware of each other's needs, and learn to meet them."*

It seems simple enough, but very, very hard to do on a consistent basis. You have to want to make your marriage work to get started down this road. We have appreciated Dr. Harley's work so much because he has helped us in our marriage to identify the basic needs that each of us has and how different the needs of a man and a woman are. Even though we have some underlying similarities, we also have some dramatic differences as individuals in what each one needs to be happy in marriage. Dr.

Harley goes on to state,

> When a man and woman marry, they share high expectations. They commit themselves to meeting certain intense and intimate needs in each other on an exclusive basis. Each agrees to "forsake all others," giving each other the exclusive right to meet these intimate needs. That does not imply that all needs are to be met by a spouse, but there are a few basic needs that most of us strictly reserve for the marriage bond. Most people expect their spouses to meet these special needs, since they have agreed not to allow anyone else to meet them (*His Needs, Her Needs,* Willard F. Harley, Jr., pp. 9-10).

Some may think that Dr. Harley's list is simplistic, but in our survey of many married couples, we found it to match up to reality. Here again are the two sets of five categories that have surfaced as the basic needs of a man and a woman in marriage.

The man's five most basic needs in marriage are:

1   Sexual fulfillment
2   Recreational companionship
3   Attractive spouse
4   Domestic support
5   Admiration

The woman's five most basic needs in marriage are:

1   Affection
2   Conversation
3   Honesty and openness
4   Financial support
5   Family commitment

What happens when these needs are not met? Many things happen, ranging from mild dissatisfaction on one end of the continuum, all the way to affairs and possibly divorce on the other end. One thing is certain: a marriage where the needs are not being met will be an unhappy one. Somehow the spouses will either look elsewhere to get those needs met, or remain in great misery, loneliness, and isolation with unfulfilled needs. Dr. Harley warns:

> In marriages that fail to meet those needs, I have seen, strikingly and alarmingly, how consistently married people choose the same pattern to satisfy their unmet needs: the extramarital affair. People wander into affairs with astonishing regularity, in spite of whatever strong, moral or religious convictions they may hold. Why? Once a spouse lacks fulfillment in any of the five needs, it creates a thirst that must be quenched. If changes do not take place within the marriage to care for that need, the individual will face the powerful temptation to fill it outside of marriage.
>
> In order to make our marriages affair proof, we cannot hide our heads in the sand. The spouse who believes his or her partner is "different," and despite unmet needs, would never take part in an affair, may receive a devastating shock some day. Instead, we need to understand the warning signs that an affair could happen, how such liaisons may begin, and how to strengthen the weak areas of a marriage in the face of such a relationship (*His Needs, Her Needs,* Willard F. Harley, Jr., pp. 9-11).

Some of you who are reading these words have a marriage that has already gone down this road of extramarital affairs. It has destroyed your faith; it has wounded you; and it has created great barriers between the two of you. Please consider the help that Dr. Harley can offer, and believe that healing and restoration are possible. We have several dear friends—married couples—who have gone down this road of affairs to the edge of the cliff of divorce and come back to survive and rebuild a trusting, fulfilling marriage. It can be done if there is a commitment on both of your parts to learn your love languages and how to meet each other's needs.

Top 10 Tip

Let Her Let Go of It

"When women talk something out in detail, somewhere along the line they let go of it. But unless they do this, they keep holding on."

—Dr. Jim Smith, *Learning to Live with the One You Love*

How Close Do You Want to Be?

A Harvard University research project brought out some startling differences as observed in young boys and girls at play. The girls' games were always shorter than the boys' games. They also noticed that the little boys preferred games with lots of rules. The boys appeared to have about as much fun discussing infractions of the rules as they did actually playing the game. In the little girls' games, if there was a quarrel, the girls were more likely to end the game rather than risk a fracture in the relationship. The girls apparently felt that *relationships* were more important than *rules*.

There is some humor in this when you look at it on the surface, but deep within this apparently latent difference between males and females is the potential for feelings of rejection, severe pain, and growing distance. In a marriage, this difference can be the root of a spouse's needs not being understood and not met.

Early in our marriage I couldn't understand myself well enough to explain why I did not feel close to Hans—all seemed to be well between us. Sometimes for no apparent reason, when Hans would be ready and interested, I just could *not* consider sharing sexual intimacy. Usually, we'd go for a walk or just talk it out, and then feelings of distance would surface in me. As I shared and Hans listened, issues sometimes large, but usually small, often would surface. As I "off-loaded" those issues and listened to Hans' feedback, his caring and listening were key to restoring in me a sense of intimacy. As a woman, I needed him to know my thoughts and feelings, and I needed to know his. I needed for him to just *want* to be with me and listen, hold hands, hug, and *be close*. A woman needs to talk it out and "let go" in order to be finished with a given topic before she can move on emotionally. Here too, Dr. Smith offers some great insight:

> When women talk something out in detail, somewhere along the line they let go of it. But unless they do this, they keep holding on. Any man who doesn't grasp that is doomed to keep on hitting the same communication wall over and over again. I can tell you that it took me only twenty years to learn this about my wife. Since then I've observed it in most women. There's something that happens in women that doesn't go on in men.
>
> The husband says, "Let's drop it. Let it alone. We've already hacked that thing to pieces." But the wife doesn't see it that way. And if hubby doesn't let her discuss it and clear the air, it will come up again!
>
> That reminds me of the man who said, "When my wife and I get into an argument, she gets historical!" *(Learning to Live with the One You Love)*

Being a Responder

I see in myself, and other women I have known, a common trait of "responder." Please understand me—I know and believe that in many areas of our lives, women are initiators, including marriage. Anyone who knows me well, knows that I am *no doormat* who waits around to jump and respond to Hans' initiative. So what am I saying? In the area of a woman's needs, and her walking through the days and months of her life, I believe this area is often overlooked, whether because of denial (out of fear of being "politically incorrect") or simply due to oversight.

Here is what I am saying: I *respond* to Hans. When *he* is on target with God's commands set forth in Scripture (1 Peter 3 and Eph.. 5) and is seeking to daily care about me in my world as a woman and wife, I will *respond*—that is, I will *naturally* be more what he needs and wants me to be as a companion, friend, and lover. It is true! Here is how he tunes into my frequency (and I'm telling you, I respond when he's tuned in these ways). By his:

- supporting me (backing me up in my authority with the kids; appreciating the pressures I face in my own job).

- **respecting what I do** (1) in the home, by joining in the care of the food, clothes, kids, cars, and so on—even the smallest gesture can make a world of difference; and (2) in my work, by recognizing that it has as much value to me as his does to him.

- **giving me warm affection**—physical touch, occasional cards, flowers, and so on . . . even when sex isn't going to happen.

- **sharing home responsibilities**—taking the initiative to share in everything related to the daily life of a household.

- **listening to me**—asking questions and digging deeper to find out where I am.

- **sharing with me**—allowing me to be *close* to him by his communication of *his* world to me.

If men would tune in to these things, I truly believe, they would be *shocked* at the changes in their wives! Their wives will *respond* to them in ways they would never have anticipated or even hoped for. Men, do you really want your wife to be there for you in your greatest needs, including sexual intimacy? Then I

Randy Finally Turned on His Radar

Randy could tell that Jamie was at the end of her rope. Their two children had been sick on and off all winter, and the middle of the night interruptions were getting to her. Night after night of interrupted sleep can be a living nightmare even in the daytime when the exhaustion gets deeper and deeper.

Finally, one night it got through to Randy that Jamie was on the brink of collapsing. Isn't it amazing what it takes for husbands to finally see that their wives are on the edge—maybe even over the edge and clinging on for dear life. Without her suggesting it, Randy told Jamie that evening, as their little Kari was again very ill, that he would stay up with her all night. For a guy, this is a real act of love since they don't genetically come by the mothering instinct. What Jamie told us was this: "He really showed me what a great husband and father he is. He not only stayed up with her and held her all night, but he also mothered me so I could truly get a deep night's sleep."

challenge you to tune in to hers! Try out this list on a consistent basis. Your wife will be a happier woman. She will be less crabby and irritable (I'm not going to guarantee "never"); and you will hear less complaining from her about her work. Although the weight of her responsibilities may not lessen on a regular basis by the changes you make, she will better be able to cope with and even enjoy her varying roles.

Hero Husbands We Know

Johnny Miller is the pastor of Calvary Church in Lancaster, Pennsylvania, and a personal friend of ours. He and his wife, Jeannie, have one of those special marriages that has stood the test of time and come out strong on the other side of the child-rearing years. He qualifies with flying colors for our hero husband award as one who has learned to tune into the frequency of his wife.

Early in their marriage, with young children in their home, Johnny saw how easily marital intimacy could slip away. He says,

> How true is the television commercial for oil filters, which says, "Pay me now, or pay me later." It's cheaper and easier to maintain an engine than to rebuild it. That's also true of marriage. Intimacy is both the process and product of maintaining a marriage, and it's cheaper than trying to rebuild. Quality time with Jeannie became a premium for me as a young pastor when I discovered I was beginning to get more intellectual and emotional stimulation from both the women and men of the church than with my own wife.
>
> I saw other women only when they were at their best. They listened appreciatively, discussed intelligently. My

own wife was too busy with babies to sense my desires, and we were both too stressed out by the growth of the church to have time just for living.

An alarm was going off in my heart. So I arranged a two-day trip alone with Jeannie and confessed what was going on inside. I said that the reason for getting it out into the open was because of my total commitment to her alone. I knew it would hurt her, and it did. It hurt me, too. We don't enjoy causing pain, but pain is sometimes the can opener to get the good stuff out.

After our tears and talking, we made some commitments to each other that have lasted twenty years. We committed to have at least one 2-hour session weekly when we would be totally alone, look each other in the eye and talk about everything on our hearts. We began to take annual retreats for spiritual and emotional refreshment, and for planning the best use of our time. We had frequent prayer times alone.

We learned to tell the children that they could not butt in when Mom and Dad were talking—something they never did comprehend, but which they learned to respect. They also learned to appreciate our dates and our joy in each other. I am sure that gave them a great deal of security as well.

Johnny and Jeannie have a beautiful relationship. Their closeness is obvious. How rare and powerful are his closing words on the intimacy they enjoy: "I still feel as excited about my sweetheart as I did more than 36 years ago when I first winked at her at a friend's wedding. There is no one on earth who knows me better, or to whom I feel closer, or with whom I would rather spend time. The work of developing intimacy with both her and with God has been worth it" ("Intimacy and Bucket Seats," *Columbia International University Quarterly,* Winter 1996, pp. 1-2).

Putting Principles into Practice

One thing we would recommend is getting away from time to time as a couple to debrief on your relationship. This way there is concentrated time to really listen to each other. Hans and I try to get away for at least one overnight without the children every quarter. Sometimes we are able to manage more than just one night, but at a minimum we need a couple of serious debriefs each year, and some great dates in between.

What amazes us is how many couples never get away from the children to work on their relationship. We have friends who never use baby-sitters and have never once gone on an overnight alone since the children were born. And then they wonder why nothing is left when the children are grown and gone!

It is not shirking your responsibility before God to have some time away from the kids occasionally. It is, in fact, one of the best things you can do *for your kids.* When you are alone, here are a few questions that you might want to discuss to get the conversation flowing, with the goal in mind of husbands tuning in to the frequency of their wives:

Personal Retreat Questions

1 On a scale of 1-10 with 1 being weak and 10 being strong, how would you rate our marital relationship? Why did you rate it the way you did?

2 What are some things you would love to do as a woman? What would you like to become that you are not right now? Be specific and let me know some of your hidden dreams.

3 On a scale of 1-10, how would you rate my sensitivity to your needs? Am I a good communicator? How can I improve? Why do you rate me the way you do?

4 What do I do in the home that is a help to you and pleases you? What do I neglect that bothers you the most?

5 If there were one thing you could change about me, what would it be?

6 What are some of the greatest hurts that you carry? What are some of your biggest fears? What about frustrations? Be open with me.

Chapter

5

Treat Her As Equal Partner

Share Leadership in the Home

Marriage is a partnership, not a dictatorship.

Today we find many people talking about the shifting paradigms of decision-making in the home. Much of it has to do with women's roles in the work force.

The biblical picture of submission, as it relates to marriage, is always coupled with our submission to Jesus Christ.

Whatever else it may be, submission is not where the wife willingly becomes a rug her husband can wipe his feet on. Neither is it where the husband is barking orders and the wife jumps in fear at the sound of his voice.

5 Treat Her As Equal Partner
Share Leadership in the Home

In a report in *Good Housekeeping* magazine, we discovered
that many people are talking about the shifting paradigms
of decision-making in the home today. Much of it has to do
with women's roles in the work force. Women are well educated
today and working in all kinds of careers. Most women who are
at home full-time are there by choice, not because they are
expected to be the one at home. Life has accelerated almost out
of control in America, and with that reality, partnership in
decision making and all home responsibilities must be shared.
According to a groundbreaking study released by the Families
and Work Institute, women earn half or more of the income in
an astonishing 44 percent of dual-earner homes. And recent
figures from the U.S. Bureau of Labor Statistics show that 22
percent of women make more than their husbands. The magazine article goes on to conclude:

> The numbers reveal a sea of change in American socie-
> ty that is turning the traditional family upside down.
> And more than money is at issue. When wives are the
> main providers, couples are forced to rethink the way
> they make decisions and take care of their children. For
> most couples, that means power shifts, negotiation, and
> sacrifice. Some husbands—and wives—feel humiliated
> or disappointed because they are not living the lives they
> are expected to. Others feel emancipated by the

changes, preferring to share the rewards and responsibilities of supporting a family, to being locked into old stereotypes (*Good Housekeeping,* January 1996, p. 93).

Hans and I operate our lives as a team. Although I am home full time, I have a demanding home business that I manage along with my responsibilities for our home and children. Another factor in our home life has been that Hans' work requires travel. That has been our reality since we have had children. In spite of his heavy travel schedule, we have negotiated a workable program to share the load as we manage our lives and large family.

Hans has always been actively involved with the kids from birth! We both shared the load when he was home with things like changing diapers, dishes, and other domestic duties. Although Hans manages the finances in our household, we make all major financial decisions together; we both take responsibility for care in our spending. I arrange for the upkeep of our family van and have done the research and purchasing of some of the major household items. We split up the work and have learned to trust each other and read each other through the years.

Foundations for True Partnership

The two most important passages of Scripture that form the foundation of our view of our marriage have to do with the issue of mutual value and submission to one another:

On the issue of equal worth—Genesis 1:27: "So God created man in his own image, in the image of God he created him; male and female he created them."—This verse from the first chapter of the Bible lays the groundwork for our mutual respect for each other. We are equally created in the image of God and therefore match in all matters of worth and humanity. When it comes to worth, we know that although there is an authority structure in our home, it in no way lessens the value and contribution of each member of the family.

On the issue of mutual submission—Ephesians 5:21-25: "Submit to one another out of reverence for Christ. Wives, submit to your husbands as to the Lord. For the husband is the head of the wife as Christ is the head of the church, his body, of which he is the Savior. Now as the church submits to Christ, so also wives should submit to their husbands in everything. Husbands, love your wives, just as Christ loved the church and gave himself up for her."—In this passage revisited once again, we point out that it begins with mutual submission. Following the admonition to "be filled with the Spirit" earlier in Ephesians 5:18, Paul showed that a couple walking in the Spirit will lovingly submit with care and concern for the needs of one another.

So how do these principles make our marriage a team? To summarize these two bottom-line operating principles of our marriage, we believe that:

We are both of equal value and worth before God and have equal weight in our marriage.

Although Hans is responsible before God as the leader of our home, we will submit to one another's needs as we walk in the Spirit out of reverence for Christ.

How Does Mutual Submission Really Work?

Submission is a topic that has already been covered very well in many Christian books. Although the subject is a hot topic, our purpose here is not to go into the depths of that discussion. We do, however, want to be sure to convey our view of what submission is not. Simply put, it is not where the wife willingly becomes a rug her husband can wipe his feet on. Neither is it where the husband gives the orders and the wife jumps in fear at the sound of his voice.

As it relates to a Christian marriage, the biblical picture of submission is always coupled with our submission to Jesus Christ. We all need authority in our lives. This is God's plan. If we are committed Christians, Jesus Christ is to be the Lord of our lives. We willingly and joyfully submit to Him because we trust and love Him; we know He has our best interests at heart. The submission that a wife is to have to her husband is to be like that.

The Portrayal of a Woman in the Bible
by Charles Swindoll

After reading all through the scriptures while looking at a woman's role, Swindoll concluded:

"Except in a few isolated and special occasions, the women who appear in the Scripture are competent, secure, qualified people who had responsible roles to fill and in doing so played a vital part in shaping of history and in the development of lives. They are beautiful examples of humanity at every economic level of society."

From *Woman: A Person of Worth & Dignity,* by Charles Swindoll, p. 9

This kind of submission is similar to what I described in Chapter Four regarding the way in which I respond to Hans. As Hans follows the Lord and obeys God in caring for my needs and in seeking to lead lovingly our family in spiritual growth, I willingly come alongside him in agreement. Together we move ahead in decisions.

Never in our marriage has it been necessary for Hans to exercise his leadership in our home by telling me I need to go a certain way on an issue. Nevertheless, as a Christian wife, I view him as the one whom God holds ultimately responsible for us as a couple and a family.

We work through situations mutually respecting the input and point of view of the other. As a matter of fact, Hans has come to realize my more feminine point of view and womanly intuition as one of his greatest assets. Because my very strengths and people skills are his weakest points, he deeply values and seeks out my insights on most situations. In that way, we both "wear the pants" in our family. Just as we experience a great security and strength as believers because of our trust in the Lord and His love for us, wives can know the same joy in this kind of mutual submissive, giving relationship with their husbands.

We need to remember the impact our success or failure in this area has on our kids. They learn by our example for better or worse. They will model their own marriages after ours. If the husband is "lording it" over his wife either by quietly refusing to listen to her point of view or openly confronting her "rebellion" with his "superior" viewpoint, he is wrong. If the wife berates her husband in front of others (especially the children), or if she quietly goes her own way refusing to consider her husband's desires, but instead does her own thing, she is wrong. They will both reap what they sow.

Paul put it best: "Wives, submit to your husbands, as is fitting in the Lord. Husbands, love your wives and do not be harsh with them" (Col. 3:18-19). Then he continued, "since you know that you will receive an inheritance from the Lord as a reward. It is the Lord Christ you are serving" (v. 24).

Decision-Making Partners

Perhaps the best way for us to explain how we practice this type of "mutual respect decision-making" is to tell the story of a major life decision we had to make a few years ago. It was one of the biggest career/life moves we have ever made. Looking back at it now, we realize that how we made the decision is almost as important to us as the decision we actually made. We were equal stakeholders in the process, and when it was finally a done deal, we both had (and continue to have) a great peace in that decision as the right one.

Decision-making for us has had a different face each time we've made a big one. We believe we've grown in this area through the years of our marriage. One of the most difficult and important decisions of our life came to us as we sensed that God was obviously closing the chapter of our years of work in Eastern Europe. We were living in Vienna, Austria at the time. For some reason, just as we were realizing that it was clearly time to move on to a new job and a new challenge, we received at least five strong feelers for new opportunities. Although we'd not indicated we were ready to move on, these organizations sought us out just at that time. They were all viable options with exciting possibilities for both of us.

Our usual practice of talking through the details and praying through the options was a part of this decision-making process. But one difference was that we needed to keep many of the details of the opportunities completely confidential. This made seeking wise counsel very limited. Furthermore, Hans had made a commitment that whatever choice we made would be the very best one for me, especially, and for the children as well. Our years in Vienna had not given me many opportunities outside of our home. So we consulted together on all the angles of each option, and Hans made very clear to me that in this particular decision we would not consider anything unless it would offer me the greatest potential to use my gifts. As he expressed it to me, his basic attitude was: "This is a decision we both have to make in our heart of hearts. I will not talk you into anything."

As we shared together, Hans came to describe each option as different "rafts" floating on the lake of our life. One by one, over a period of about three months, three of the five rafts became burdened down with weights (various negative reasons) and sank out of the running . We were then left with two floating rafts. Each was highly desirable. One of the organizations flew Hans back to the U.S. for an in-depth interview. He was also able to visit the other one, and he came back to Vienna very sure deep inside which one was right for us. But I had no idea he knew! At that point, just between him and the Lord, Hans decided he would not tell me but would trust the Lord to place in my heart the right one as well. I was actually leaning toward the one he was not inclined to take, but was still open to both.

As the process was heating up for a deadline, we set aside two days to seek God's will with prayer and fasting, promising not to speak of the decision again until we'd completed those two set-aside days. Finally, we drove to a beautiful park in Vienna—where we could be alone without distractions—to share our hearts deeply once again. During those two days, the Lord brought together for me some reading and Scripture to clearly confirm His leading in this decision. As we sat together in our van in the pouring rain, Hans asked me which option I believed was the one the Lord had for us. I told him my conclusion. It was the same as his—not my original inclination. He told me then and only then that he had been convinced of it for several weeks. But his attitude was that only if God showed me directly would we walk through the door together.

I can't express clearly enough how powerful it was to me that Hans *honored* my needs and *respected* my insights. He also demonstrated faith in the Lord to entrust me to Him and showed honor for my own walk with the Lord by leaving things in His hands. He refused to manipulate me or place his own position and calling above the plans the Lord would have for me in our next place of ministry.

They're Not All Heroes

We have tried to focus each chapter on a "Hero Husband" to lend a positive slant to a book that might appear to be "husband bashing." We will do the same later in this chapter. First, however, we also want to share a true story of a couple we have known who have had a tragic marriage that did not turn out well. Many details have been altered to protect their privacy. Though worse than some, this story personifies the destruction to a marriage and home when a husband and wife do not live according to the plan God has designed as we just described—not with submission, respect, yielded love, and consideration, but with selfishness, rebellion, harshness, and bitterness. It reminds us of Proverbs 17:22: "A cheerful heart is good medicine, but a crushed spirit dries up the bones."

Mandy and Brent were married for twelve years. They have two children, an eleven-year-old son, and a nine-year-old daughter.

They met in their church singles group. They grew close as they worked together in music, enjoying the gifts of each other, and admiring what they saw in each other. They soon began a dating relationship. Things were a bit rocky from the start for them, but they wrote it off to their mutually strong personalities. Before long Brent proposed and Mandy accepted. Even so, doubts plagued Mandy. Her parents' marriage had ended in divorce. Brent was just happy to have the exclusive love of Mandy; she was quite a "catch" for him. Their singles leader and other friends warned them to wait awhile before getting married. Putting all advice and doubts aside, however, Brent and Mandy married the following summer.

Within the first year, both Brent and Mandy knew they had made a big mistake. The very concerns that had aroused doubt in Mandy were now her life. Brent, whose brother and father had died when he was a baby, was the only child of a widowed mother. He soon resented any outside interests and friends Mandy had, feeling jealous of her time and love. Their previous goal of working in music together had quickly evaporated. Brent had decided not to pursue further education and refused to see Mandy pursue her professional goals. Giving up on his own previous goals, he decided instead to try his hand at selling automobiles. As a moody and mostly self-absorbed man, he was not able to make a living at sales.

Their two children had arrived much too quickly for both of them. Mandy tried to help make ends meet by waitressing a few times a week, but the resentment between them was thick. Brent complained that Mandy didn't "support" him and would not "submit" to his leadership. Mandy struggled with Brent's expectations that she treat him as the king of her world. He withheld love as punishment for her lack of submission and service toward him. Brent left most of the child care and training to Mandy, only relating to the kids as a doting daddy, with pet names that suited babies and toddlers, but which quickly grew old, along with the kids.

The years went by. Both Mandy and Brent grudgingly accepted their lot together since, as committed Christians, divorce was not an option for either of them. But their marriage had become a cold war. The bitterness each felt for the other in their own minds, they attributed to the other's failure to *obey Scripture*. Brent convinced himself that their whole problem from day one had been Mandy's refusal to "submit" to him. To him, she was living in sin since she had rebelled against his "leadership." Mandy, on the other hand, was sure Brent was incapable of ever loving her as Christ loved the church. He was too busy loving himself and correcting her and the kids to actually love them. His harshness and sharp comments cut Mandy deeply.

In their eleventh year of marriage, Mandy fell seriously ill. Mandy knew she needed emotional and spiritual healing as well as physical healing. She and Brent agreed to go for marriage counseling. They found a wonderful counselor with whom they could both be open. But the bitter years and pain had done profound damage.

None of us knows how much the pain of a crushed spirit contributed to Mandy's illness, but Scripture clearly does correlate emotional and spiritual health with physical health. We cannot expect to live with anger, pain, resentment, and hurt forever without eventual consequences. This painful story should put up warning signals to all of us. We hope it gives you pause to "stop, look, listen, and seek."

Stop: Are you struggling with each other in the area of submission?

Look: Review Ephesians 5 to check your marriage against the truth of God's Word. Are you willing to give and love your spouse and not demand your own way? Have you allowed distance and coldness to grow?

Listen: Ask your spouse, How do you view our roles in our marriage and home? Men, ask: Am I too demanding or harsh with you? Do you feel that I "lord it over you" in our marriage? What changes would help you most? Women, ask: Do you sense my respect for you? What could I do to honor you as my husband? What changes would help you most?

Seek: Professional help from a biblical counselor if your marriage is on the rocks.

Remember Ephesians 4:26-27: "'In your anger do not sin': Do not let the sun go down while you are still angry, and do not give the devil a foothold." Dr. Paul Meier, respected psychiatrist, author, and godly husband, makes a powerful statement about these verses. In the many years of his practice as a doctor of body and mind, he has found that many diseases, including cancer, are "caused by not obeying this clear command of Scripture." Anger is meant to be dealt with. If it is not, it will eventually weaken the immune system, and illness will result!

If we allow anger to rule us, we will be in danger of giving Satan grounds against us through our unforgiving spirit. He will seek to use that anger to further damage our relationships and us (v. 27).

Hero Husbands We Know

Now on to a more encouraging story—a scenario with the same potential for destruction, but with a much brighter outcome. David and Jenny are both highly talented individuals. In their early years of marriage both had impressive jobs in corporate America. They both had their places to flourish; they enjoyed their life together immensely. David, strongly driven in his job, was also disciplined in managing their good income.

Several years later they decided to start their family. When their daughter arrived, they agreed they wanted Jenny to stay at home to raise her. Within weeks of the arrival of their baby, David and Jenny made a major move for David's career. The difficulty of adjusting to new motherhood was compounded for Jenny by the shock of a totally new environment, having left that of her career. She had a tough time. David's success and responsibilities went on, but he was taken by surprise at the struggle Jenny was facing. His high-powered, successful wife was showing new sensitivities and needs. Yet he plowed ahead full bore, placing some expectations upon Jenny that she could not meet. Although David believed (at least in theory) in loving Jenny, respecting her in her new role, and sharing all decision-making with her, Jenny did not feel those things from him. They had some painful times and misunderstandings, and sometimes the state of their marriage discouraged them deeply.

So what changed the situation? David and Jenny simply had commitment in their marriage. That commitment was what pushed them to find answers to the misunderstandings and to make needed changes during a difficult time in their marriage. David arranged to go with his friend to Promise Keepers. Even after the birth of their son, things continued to improve. David was a great father, and was growing in understanding of his responsibility to meet the needs of his wife. Their godly pastor recommended "Marriage Encounter," as he had seen the tremendous results the marriage retreat had produced in many marriages. David and Jenny scheduled the weekend, not really knowing what to expect. They returned to tell us that their marriage had been transformed. They even asked us to please recommend "Marriage Encounter" in this book.

We consider David a "hero husband." Unlike so many men who are unwilling to consider their need to change and grow, David sought out excellent resources. David opened his life to these lessons. He has grown markedly in his ability to respond well as he has sought the Lord for His help. He's been a testimony to those who know him in his loving relationship to his wife, Jenny. David continues to move out of some of his more natural patterns with obvious positive results. He and Jenny are a very effective team whose commitment to growth make them sharper than ever because of their great gifts!

Putting Principles into Practice

For Husbands:

Your position of leadership in the home comes with a great deal of responsibility. Do not use your place for dictatorship but for leadership in your partnership with your wife.

For Wives:

Consider how you can support your husband in difficult decisions as a team player. If you find that you live in a difficult marriage situation, pray for grace to do what is right, and pray for him that God will change his wrongful attitudes.

For Both of You:

Think about some of the issues raised in this chapter and write down your own convictions about them. Here are several questions to ponder:

- In our marriage, do we view the husband as being the leader of the home?

  If so, why? In what ways do we mean that he is the leader?

  If not, why not?

- What does it mean for a couple to submit to one another? (Eph..5:21-25)

- As the leader of the home, what is the man's unique responsibility before God to fulfill that role?

- In the issue of submission for the woman, what does the Bible (as in Eph.. 5) mean when it asks wives to submit to their husbands? What does this mean in real life in your marriage?

Chapter 6

Walk a Mile in Her Shoes

Understand the World of Your Wife

Few men take the initiative to really walk in their

wives' shoes, even for a full day.

Men and women have entirely different views of reality when it comes to those moments when they arrive home from work in the evening.

The best medicine I ever take to help me appreciate Donna's world is to switch roles with her for a few days.

A man's understanding and true caring for his wife will grow proportionately to how well he sees life from her point of view.

6 Walk a Mile in Her Shoes
Understand the World of Your Wife

Jenny was newly married to a man nine years her senior. Their house had been his "bachelor pad." She made it into a nice home. She worked at a dentist's office and he as an accountant. When they conceived their first child, she worked part time until their son arrived. At that point life changed dramatically for Jenny! As many first-time moms do, she quit her job to be home full time with her son.

Jenny was lonely, tied down to the house, and busy trying to manage household demands along with a new baby. Tom continued his routine just as he always had, committed to all of his same outside activities. He continued to golf, take a couple nights a week for his bowling, as well as weekends away fishing with the guys. Even after their second son arrived, he never paused to consider what Jenny's life was like.

In spite of our more liberated age, many men live as Tom has. He assumes that, as the provider, he is doing his part for his family. He wonders "what *does* Jenny *do* all day?" Tom never considers trying to walk in her shoes or even laying aside some of his bachelor habits. He has it great! At least according to him he does.

But what about Jenny? For a long time she carried on, did it all, and put up with all of his absences. Many women in her situation would have either fallen into an affair, or else struggled along, growing bitter at being misunderstood and forced to basically raise the children alone. Jenny, however, had come to faith in Christ through a local Bible study. She found friendship and encouragement from other young mothers. As she grew in the Lord, she not only tried to share Christ with Tom, but she also sought to grow closer to him in their marriage.

One of the best things Jenny did was to begin to *give* Tom more responsibility for their kids. She would set up occasional evenings to leave the kids with Tom and take the night off to enjoy an evening with friends. She would arrange baby-sitting so she and Tom could go out together. Jenny has found ways to adjust and grow, but still, overall, she often feels as though Tom doesn't truly appreciate her.

Pulling Up the Drawbridge?

To contrast how men and women view those moments when they come home from work in the evening, listen to this humorous description by Jim Smith in his book, *Learning to Live with the One You Love:*

Top **10** Tip
Reverse Roles Once a Year

From a Southern California Dad:

"At least once a year I ask my wife to take off and go see her parents or spend the weekend with some of her girlfriends. And while she's gone, I try to take care of the home front as she likes so that she wouldn't be too discouraged at the mess she might finds upon her return. This accomplishes two purposes in our marriage:

She gets her batteries recharged, with some needed rest and a change of pace.

I get to be reminded what her life is like, which helps greatly when we live our normal roles and inevitable conflicts arise."

The average man comes home believing that, having put in a hard day at work, it is now his God-given right to retire to his castle. He now wishes to enter his castle, pull up the drawbridge, and let the alligators swim in the moat. He is not particularly thrilled when he learns that there are some alligators loose in the castle.

Now a woman's idea of an evening well spent is called "sharing"—in detail. The career woman wants to share her day with her husband—in detail—and the home-maker wants to share war stories from the home front. And what about the woman who has little children at home and has not been out of the house? She has been locked up with the "Viet Cong" all day and can't wait to turn them over to him the minute he walks in the door. She would like to have an adult conversation—in detail—with her husband (pp. 34-35).

Have you ever noticed that most men think they have spent a meaningful evening at home with their wives if they have simply been under the same roof? No conversation, no dialogue, no give and take, but they're there, in the same place at the same time—he thinks that means "closeness."

A man wants his wife to behave more or less like a golden retriever; that is, she should come around occasionally and pass through the room, letting him acknowledge and pat her. Then she should go on doing whatever she was doing, coming back in about an hour to let him pat and acknowledge her again. If she does that, he feels that he has spent a wonderful, warm evening with her. So when she complains, "You never spend any time with me," he's shocked. "What?" he yells. "I've been home all week." Hyperbole? Hopefully for most of us this is at least something of an exaggeration. But the point is nonetheless true.

A couple in Nebraska wrote to us about their typical exchange in the evening after work (they both work outside the home): "I'll come home, and she'll ask me how my day went. I'm tired and ready for a change of pace—not wanting to talk about what I just left behind—so I'll answer with that great four-letter word that is good for almost any occasion: *fine*." For a man this is a signal that he does not want to talk. But she is not satisfied. Our friend goes on, "She wants more details. She wants to know what happened, what discussions I had today, what big decisions I made, what plans I made for our future. Although I know she is not asking for *every* detail of my day, I do find it exhausting to basically have to rehearse the whole day again. Perhaps I could record my day, and she could listen to the tape!"

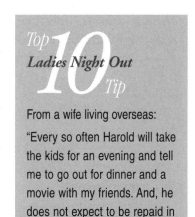

Top **10** *Tip*
Ladies Night Out

From a wife living overseas:
"Every so often Harold will take the kids for an evening and tell me to go out for dinner and a movie with my friends. And, he does not expect to be repaid in kind with his friends. That really means a lot to me."

This husband identified very succinctly the need a woman feels with her life mate—that need for intimate communication at the end of every day. Furthermore, my friend wrote this in our questionnaire about his wife's number one need: "I believe my wife's number one need is for me to communicate or talk *more* with her." Again the knowing is there, it is the energy that often fails.

Of Noble Character

Let's take a closer look at the life of a woman. And for a moment let's glimpse into Proverbs 31, where the Bible gives us the picture of "The Wife of Noble Character." This passage written centuries ago may seem at first pass, totally detached from the realities of modern life. But as with all of Scripture, there is a gold mine of wisdom and practical application if you look carefully:

A wife of noble character who can find? She is worth far more than rubies. Her husband has full confidence in her and lacks nothing of value. She brings him good, not harm, all the days of her life. She selects wool and flax and works with eager hands. She is like the merchant ships, bringing her food from afar. She gets up while it is still dark; she provides food for her family and portions for her servant girls. She considers a field and buys it; out of her earnings she plants a vineyard. She sets about her work vigorously; her arms are strong for her tasks. She sees that her trading is profitable, and her lamp does not go out at night. In her hand she holds the distaff and grasps the spindle with her fingers. She opens her arms to the poor and extends her hands to the needy. When it snows, she has no fear for her household; for all of them are clothed in scarlet. She makes coverings for her bed; she is clothed in fine linen and purple. Her husband is respected at the city gate, where he takes his seat among the elders of the land. She makes linen garments and sells them, and supplies the merchants with sashes. She is clothed with strength and dignity; she can laugh at the days to come. She speaks with wisdom, and faithful instruction is on her tongue.

She watches over the affairs of her household and does not eat the bread of idleness. Her children arise and call her blessed; her husband also, and he praises her: "Many women do noble things, but you surpass them all." Charm is deceptive, and beauty is fleeting; but a woman who fears the Lord is to be praised. Give her the reward she has earned, and let her works bring her praise at the city gate (Prov. 31:10-31).

For many women this picture is actually depressing. The qualities and gifts of this woman are praised and lifted up to be our goal to seek as wives and mothers. But how? But when? Is this what we women really even want today? I (Donna) remember how encouraging it was for me to learn that this woman was most likely at least in her fifties! It took time for her to develop the many areas of work and productiveness she is praised for. I do want her traits, but I don't know if I will reach them any time soon.

Guys, perhaps your wife is a young woman with your first young child, or she may be the mother of many children of varying ages. Whether she is home full time, juggling part-time work, or has a full-time career, it is likely that the bulk of home responsibility falls on her shoulders! I'm telling you, managing it all is overwhelming!

Honestly, now, you often don't truly understand all that is involved in homemaking, do you. Perhaps you take your wife for granted, knowingly or unknowingly. Wherever you may stand, the constant, never-ending management of household duties is invisible to many men. They assume that their wives are just fine with the way things are. So duties fall to her alone, in spite of the fact that marriage is to be a partnership. "Appreciation" and "gratefulness" are far from the minds of most men when they think of what their wives do to carry the load at home.

Let's go back to Ephesians 5:25, 28, and 33—remember that the command to the husband is to *love* his wife? One of the most powerful ways to love her is to *show her you appreciate her and are deeply grateful for all she does each day.* In fact, Peter exhorts, "Husbands, in the same way *be considerate* as you live with your wives" (1 Peter 3:7). Why? Because God commands it? Yes! But also because of the *reward* you will receive by seeking to enter into her world.

The Wages of Love

Whether or not they were employed outside the home, nine out of ten women surveyed by the Families and Work Institute said it was their responsibility to take care of their families. And according to another study, women who *out-earn* their husbands do even *more* housework by a large margin than women who make about the same as their husbands:

> Even when women earn more, men rarely contribute their share at home—another major source of tension. When any of her three children gets sick, Lisa, a pathologist, is the one who takes a day off—even though her husband, George, a computer programmer, earns a third of what she does. "All of a sudden my work is secondary," she says (*Good Housekeeping,* January 1996, pp. 94-95).

Men don't seem to get the unfairness of the load that is often placed on the shoulders of women. Many women work as hard as men with little external reward. A recent article in the Denver Post underscores just how much homemakers are worth, though often underappreciated. Journalist Guy Boulton quotes Katherine Freeman, an economics professor at the University of Denver:

> By one estimate, if the work of all mothers were included in the gross domestic product (GDP), the measure of the U.S. economy would be 20 to 30 percent higher. Given that the GDP is estimated at more than $8 trillion, such work adds up to more than $1.6 trillion a year in unaccounted economic value. "We basically have unpaid labor," Freeman says. That unpaid labor isn't limited to so-called stay-at-home mothers. No matter how much a husband and wife share the burden of running a household, in most families it's not a 50-50 split. Women typically bear most of the burden. Freeman confirms, "They just tend to put in a lot more hours." (The Denver Post, May 13, 2001, by Guy Boulton, cover story.)

Walk a mile in her shoes. Try to understand as a husband just how much is on the shoulders of your wife. Remember, her efforts are equal to 20 to 30 percent of our GDP in the United States!

Respect, Respect, Respect

A lot of us men get hung up trying to be control freaks. If we are in a position of leadership where we work or at least have control over our jobs, we tend to carry that tendency of control into our wives' domains. We must learn to respect her world and the decisions she makes about those things she is responsible for. In our home we try to practice the motto, "Whoever is in charge of the task gets to decide how it will be done."

One of our "wife" friends wrote this interesting story about a battle she faced in this arena, having to do with washing the windows right before her parents came. I (Hans) have never been able to appreciate the level of emotional intensity that rises in Donna when family is coming to town. As far as I'm concerned, life should just carry on as usual until we go pick them up at the airport to bring them home. Why can't they see us the way we live every day? This is no small source of irritation between us as Donna goes into "visitors are coming to town mode."

Our friend Sara told us this story:

> This past spring I decided that I wanted the windows washed badly enough to pay someone else to do it. My parents' imminent visit was part of the motivation. I knew just whom to call, had already figured out a way to pay for it, and had placed the call. Unfortunately, the gentleman called back during dinner, and my husband answered the phone. Thinking it was a telemarketing sale, he said, "No, we don't need the windows cleaned. Thank you very much."
>
> "Honey," I exclaimed, "I called them. I want it done before Mom gets here."
>
> "We don't need to spend money on that. I'll do it, or the kids will." And so it went. You guessed it. Next week my parents had come and gone, and the windows remained dirty. The week after Paul went on a business trip, I cleaned the windows myself for "free."

And then Sara shared with us the punch line: When we asked the question, "If you could change anything about your husband, what would it be?" She answered, "Have him trust my judgment in my areas of responsibility instead of second-guessing me."

Ouch! Respect is a two-way street, and we husbands have to be willing to give it if we would like to receive it. This reminded us of one of our favorite sayings of late:

Blessed are the control freaks
for they shall inhibit the earth.

The Demanding Schedules of Work

Hans has always tried to listen when I tell him about the responsibilities I carry. As I already said, ever since we have had children, *travel* has been a part of our lives. For the first few years, Hans traveled into Eastern Europe as part of our ministry of training pastors and Christian leaders. Then for the past decade, he's traveled as the CEO of a large ministry all over the U.S. and around the world. Much of the time I have been home with our children, though now I also travel more often with my work and with Hans. We've done pretty well balancing all this travel and pressure, by keeping our other priorities straight. We make adjustments each year to the schedule to be sure we have adequate time for our marriage and family. But when friction and stress start to show up, we are forced to take the time to figure out what's gone wrong.

Through the years we have come to those times where I'm feeling discouraged by all of the various aspects of bearing the weight on the home front. We realize that the best means of *coping*—or even better, doing my job well—is to have Hans' true understanding and support. As we talk it through, he comes to realize more how much I carry and do as a homemaker. The expectations and needs of the children, their schools, activities, carpool, church, friends, and so on all weigh very heavily on the homemaker.

The intricacy of all of those demands and the "24-hour-a-day element" of it all sometimes add up to major overload for any woman. Add to those responsibilities the element of a husband away on travel, or her own job, or home business, and "Whew!" Most women say, "I've had it!" Sometimes when Hans has been on a heavy travel schedule, one more kid's asking me something or calling "Mom!" and I blurt out, "Hey, kids, that's it! I can't hear 'Mom' again. Just call 'Dad' (just so I can hear it), and I'll answer anyway."

So what is the key? How does the husband meet this need for understanding and relief in his wife? First, he must truly listen. He has to walk in her shoes and try to crawl inside her world. Ask questions to dig deeper into her life. Then he must take action to bring her relief. Men, sacrificing your own agenda is needed here in the nitty-gritty daily realities of marriage.

Husbands, try a few of these tips on for size:

- Ask her, "how are you doing today?"
- Has she had some "downtime" today?
- Come on, kids, let's go for a drive/walk/bike-ride/so on.
- I'll make dinner and do the dishes with the kids; which days would help you most?
- I understand—your day would have certainly done *me* in! It means so much to me that you take such good care of our kids and our home. Thank you.
- Pick a night this week and go out for dinner with your friends. I'll cook dinner and take care of the kids.
- Let's go out for dinner alone—just you and me.
- Let's organize a written schedule of household work that divides the responsibilities and that is fair for everyone.

Whatever you do, men, find a way to give your wife true relief. Why? Partly because you are commanded to. Remember "Love" from Ephesians 5 and "Be Considerate" from 1 Peter 3? But beyond that, you do it for the great reward of a *happy wife!* She is not going to "quit" her work. To the contrary, your true understanding will give her the joy of knowing you are truly carrying the weight with her. She'll have more joy and strength to continue each day.

A number of years ago we decided that Donna would go to Phoenix each year for a getaway week to be with her parents for a break from her daily grind. We finally realized that the weight of home responsibility *never* truly shifted off of her shoulders! Even when Donna is able to go on a ministry trip with me, or a getaway just for the two of us, the burden of childcare, meals, and so on still falls on her to arrange and carry in our absence. During the week Donna is gone to Phoenix, each year, I carry the full load at home, by myself.

Workaholism Is Anything but Healthy

Recent studies show that one reason women always seem to out-live men is because of the stress men face in their careers. It seems that even women who hold high-pressured career jobs don't internalize the work to the extent that men do.

For males, it seems that the ego is all wrapped up in work. Thus, the tendency is to become lost in the job and neglect the home front. The ironic thing here is that men would be far more healthy, balanced, and happy if they were more engaged in the domestic home side of their lives.

On those occasions when Hans has "walked in my shoes," truly carrying the responsibilities I normally carry for more than one day, he is always *shocked!* Most women feel that their husbands don't have a clue. And I must say, most husbands in America truly don't. I'm so grateful that Hans is willing to "walk in my shoes" from time to time.

Recently Hans got a firsthand reminder of all that I do. I went to bed *all day*—just one day with a sinus infection. (Most of the time I just go on, but since I had been dizzy the night before, I decided to go to bed for just one day.) That night, Hans said, "I don't believe you do it!" After just one day of dealing with four kids, their friends, questions, spats, homework, and trying to do some household jobs at the same time, he was overwhelmed. He told me to remind him of that day the next time he looked at me funny after a grueling day of sole responsibility for our family and household.

Men, loving your wife as Christ does the church sounds like an impossible standard to attain. But Christ made a much greater sacrifice by laying aside His rights and privileges as the Son of God. He is not only your example, but He also has promised to give you His power to be what you should be as a husband!

Hero Husbands We Know

Not long ago we had the chance to have Christian singer Steve Green in our home for an evening. He was in town shooting a video for our ministry, and we wanted our kids to have a chance to get to know him personally. Because Steve grew up as the child of one of our staff in Argentina, we have known his family since before he was married. His parents Charles and Jo Green served with our ministry for almost forty years in South America.

As our kids pumped Steve with questions that evening, he told us about the new travel bus he had built. Since he spends most of his life on the road, he has a big bus for his band and back-up crew. They also sleep in the bus while on the road. For several years Steve's wife, Marijean, and their two children traveled with him to all his concerts. They all lived together in their big bus. Sounds like one big happy family experience doesn't it? It was at first, but it didn't last. Life on the road gets old after a while, especially as the children get older and start school—thus the need for a new bus and new strategy.

Now Steve Green travels without Marijean and the children to most of his concerts. But they are not neglected or forgotten. He has several special things he does to make them feel important, which will remain his private family secrets. The one expression of love and understanding he practices consistently for Marijean is something that everyone who goes to his concerts knows of. In the middle of his evening program, invariably he will pick up a stage phone and talk with his wife and children live on-stage. Her voice is piped through to the audience so everyone can hear her voice and receive greetings from Marijean. While they are talking, either a video or still photos of her and the children are displayed on the large stage screen.

What is Steve communicating by all this fuss? A mountain of good will. He is letting his wife know that he is thinking about her while he is away. And he is telling her that she is important enough to him that he wants all his concert goers to know her too—*he is not the only important member of the Green family.* Finally, he is making a strong statement to the world that he is a deeply committed family man and hopelessly in love with his wife. That is good protection for a life on the road!

Walk a Mile in Her Shoes

Putting Principles into Practice

After you've walked in your wife's shoes for a while, here are some practical suggestions for using what you've learned. Take the initiative in things like kicking her out of the kitchen, taking over parental taxi service, shopping, and cleaning. Make these acts as spontaneous as possible, or better yet, make them a regular weekly part of your life. Simple action along with caring about her world will usually be *all she needs* to jump back into the "fray." Although she may still be tired, her spirits will be lifted and more ready to "charge" into her life's demands.

Hans' Tried and True Travel Tips

For the many men who travel, there is special advice for you, before you take off and after you land from your latest business trip. Travel away from home adds unique pressure to a marriage, to the husband-wife relationship, and to the role of a father with his children. Some important tips to remember along the way are these:

1 **Before you leave**

Make sure the family is taken care of. Leave your wife a detailed schedule of where you will be, what you will be doing, and how you can be reached.

Spend extra quality time with your wife and children before departure.

Don't expect a hit-and-run relationship prior to your departure to satisfy your sexual needs.

2 While you are on the road

Be sure to call your family regularly.

If your wife or family feels they need it, carry a pager or cell phone along.

Leave love notes behind for your wife and family to find.

Send mail to your family if you are gone for a longer period of time—especially if you are out of the country.

E-mail your family regular updates on your travels.

Send gifts or flowers if it is an extended trip.

Set up times to chat via the Internet with your family.

3 Take care of yourself while you are traveling

Try to maintain consistency in your personal devotions/quiet times with God.

Avoid situations that will compromise your integrity.

Try not to spend too much time alone—travel with colleagues when possible.

4 Upon reentry

Don't go straight back to work if you can help it. Your family needs you first.

Plan some travel-recovery time.

Work aggressively to debrief your wife on your travels.

Debrief with her about what happened in her life—listen!

Do the same with your children.

Don't try to cover travel guilt by showering your family with presents—what they need is some quality time with you.

7

Appreciate Her Worth

You're Living With Nobility!

It has been decades since "Leave it to Beaver," but many men are still hung up on the old traditional role of the husband and wife portrayed in the '50s.

Even when women earn more, men rarely contribute their share at home—a major source of tension in the modern marriage.

If a man's home is "his castle," he needs to treat his spouse as the *queen,* not the *maidservant!*

7 Appreciate Her Worth
You're Living With Nobility

Even though it has been decades since "Leave it to Beaver," many men today are still hung up on the old traditional view of the worth of the husband and wife. Many Baby Boomers grew up with the television models of "Ozzie and Harriett," "Father Knows Best," "Leave it to Beaver," "The Dick Van Dyke Show," and "I Love Lucy." In all of those shows, Mom was the faithful homemaker while Dad did all of the "important work" outside of the home. Mom took care of the kids, took care of the dishes, and took care of the house, while Dad was out there bringing home the paycheck and making a mark on the world.

The subtle undertone and attitude that was projected through all of those role models was that *Dad's working world was more important than Mom's*—at least what he did was more important than what she did. Today we Boomers are raising a new generation of kids who will marry with no reference point to that 1950s view of marriage. In contrast to Ozzie and Harriet, our kids are being raised on shows like "Friends," where roles and commitments are anything but traditional.

In the last chapter we looked at the need for a man to understand the world of his wife: her *role*. This chapter is about her *worth*. The working world has opened up to the woman, and we've seen "glass ceilings" shatter everywhere. We applaud this greater opportunity for women outside of the home, but that's not the full picture. Can a woman be valued and respected by what she does inside the home as a homemaker, wife, and mother? We would say the answer is a resounding yes! In fact, the trend is that more and more women are leaving the workplace and their careers by choice to go back home during the child-raising years of their marriages. The point is this: men need to own the fact that women have equal worth whether they're homemakers or CEOs.

A Woman's Worth

Let's go back to Proverbs 31 to illustrate this truth. This was one amazing woman! Everything about her demands that we give her full dignity and honor—she is a woman worthy of full respect:

Proverbs 31:10-11

A wife of noble character who can find? She is worth far more than rubies. Her husband has full confidence in her and lacks nothing of value.

Many women today are realizing that the career model for the working mother is not all that it was cracked up to be. Just as more and more families are moving back to their roots in the hometowns where they grew up, looking for a simpler life of more quality and a slower pace, women are leaving the corporate world to go back home in greater numbers. Financial realities, of course, demand that many mothers work. No matter which role your wife is most occupied with, you as her husband must learn to value and appreciate her worth.

I (Hans) have grown to appreciate more and more, as the years have gone by, the incredible worth that Donna provides in our home and marital relationship. I appreciate that she is home

We've Come a Long Way—Maybe
This is not the 1950s

Many of us grew up with the television models of "Ozzie and Harriet," "Father Knows Best," "Leave it to Beaver," "The Dick Van Dyke Show," and "I Love Lucy." In all of those shows, Mom was the faithful homemaker while Dad did all of the "important work" outside of the home.

This picture of the '50s is hardly a working model for today. Aside from being impractical, it's really not all that biblical..

raising our children and running a home business. I consider what she does just as important and valuable as what I do. She has chosen to work out of our home so she can be available to our four kids on a daily basis. I try to show her how much I value her in the following ways:

- By listening to what is going on in her life.
- By honoring her publicly whenever I have opportunity to do so.
- By communicating to our children my respect for her, I affirm that she is worthy of their respect.
- By affirming her in the decision-making areas that affect her responsibilities in our family.
- By initiating ways for her to have "vacation" away from her job just as I get vacation away from my work.
- By sending the signals every chance I get that her home business is significant

The View from Her Side

Life in America with all of its modern conveniences has accelerated the pace and expectations put upon the family. Choices bombard us constantly. This has isolated us from one another within the family, church, and community, as our lives are so busy and full. I especially remember when we first arrived back in America after living overseas for nearly ten years—how shocking it all was. Life in most other countries is slower and more family oriented. We would watch in amazement at how everyone lived in the U.S., and we wondered, "Where *are* they all going? What is all the great *hurry* about?" We soon discovered that much of the energy and time expended by people involved:

> **"Doing"**—activities such as soccer, ice skating, baseball, football, ballet, and church clubs.

> **"Going"**—to pull off all of those activities, the family van had almost become "home."

> **"Getting"**—shopping and consuming is truly an American art form. Nowhere else in the world have all of the options and availability of commercialism drawn people to buy, buy, buy. Shopping has become a recreation in America.

As the homemaker, together with Hans, we've sought to find our own way, as I know many of you have, to *not* be ruled by the standard "way it is" described above—what H. Norman Wright so aptly described as "prehysteric parenting," in his book by the same title (Victor). We seek to make our family life, relationships with our kids, and ministry our primary focus and motivation. I believe we do have a very close bond as a family, and we end up spending a lot of time at home together. Inviting the kids' friends in and opening our home to others are things we're doing more and more.

We want to make being
- a close family,
- more like our Lord Jesus Christ,
- a caring family for others in our neighborhood and church family, and
- a loving testimony of a Christian family

the priority of our lives.

Sometimes, though, reality demands that our schedule be too full, and priorities are left in the dust as I run about doing, going, and getting! That's life, and no home is perfect.

You're Living with Nobility

As a husband, I would challenge you to read through this "paraphrase" of Proverbs 31, and circle the qualities you see in your wife. Then share with her those good qualities and thank her for the initiative she takes in meeting the needs of you and the kids in those areas. Remember, the woman portrayed here most certainly grew into being the "Noble Wife" over a period of years and received much praise from her husband along the way!

Proverbs 31—A Personal Paraphrase

The "wife of noble character" is said to be rare indeed! She is of highest value and worth, and her husband totally trusts her—not second-guessing her, but rather relying on her, knowing her work will bring him good, not harm, **all the days of her life.** She is a woman with multiple skills and training, involved in commerce. She works very hard, maybe even having her own income. She is strong, compassionate, generous, given to hospitality. She plans ahead and dresses herself and her family well. She decorates her home beautifully. She exudes "strength" and "dignity," but has a sense of humor. She speaks wisely and chooses her words carefully as she instructs her children. Her husband is respected highly. Her children and husband praise her. But her highest praise is that her beauty is inward, as she is a great woman of God who walks closely with Him!

We appreciate Charles Swindoll's wrestling with the issue of a woman's worth in his booklet titled: *Woman: A Person of Worth and Dignity*. As he looks at two possible extremes today, he carefully identifies the causes for these biblically inaccurate viewpoints and sets a good balanced viewpoint.

The Dangers of Inaccurate Viewpoints

1 A misunderstanding and misapplication of "submission."

Husbands and wives alike have done this. Pastors and other authorities have also contributed to this most unfortunate problem.

2 A failure on the part of Christian husbands to carry out three essential responsibilities, namely:
to think biblically,
to lead fairly, and
to release unselfishly.

3 A strong, well-organized action from the secular world system to "liberate" today's woman . . . regardless.

Even those who don't want to be "liberated" are made to appear foolish and backward. The happy homemaker, the fulfilled woman who enjoys being at home, is mocked by the system.

4 **An equally strong resistance from some voices in Christendom to keep the Christian woman boxed in, seated, and silent.**

Frankly, I am convinced this underscores the fact that God never intended the woman to feel inferior or to live fearfully beneath some heavy cloud of unfair domination. While no one who takes Scripture seriously can deny that a wife must, indeed, fit into her husband's plans (1 Peter 3:1) and ultimately allow him the place of final authority in the home (Eph.. 5:22), in no way is she ever viewed as an individual lacking in worth or dignity (*Woman: A Person of Worth and Dignity*, Charles Swindoll, pp. 8-9).

Hero Husbands We Know

I (Hans) just returned from an encouraging trip to meet with an acquaintance we'll call William—a hero of a husband, who lives in the beautiful rolling hills of eastern Pennsylvania. Fortunately, I also had the chance to meet his lovely wife, Barb, and learn of their special relationship, especially as it involves his respect for her worth in their marriage.

William has been the president of a multinational organization for twenty-five years. Four years ago they moved their world headquarters from New Jersey to Pennsylvania. During the process of renovating their new corporate center, they added 35,000 square feet of new offices to their complex. When it came time to work on interior design, his gifted wife, Barb, volunteered to take care of all planning for the furnishings, colors, wall coverings, paintings, and decorations. Quite a big job and big commitment for his spouse! William had two choices—bring in a "professional" and pay the big bucks or take a risk and allow Barb to use her gifts in his world.

Not every woman is gifted in interior decorating, but Barb is. I spent two days at their headquarters, and I can tell you that it is beautiful beyond description. Tastefully and professionally done, Barb left her mark on the world where her husband rules as chief executive. William's decision to ask Barb to bring her gifts into his world in such a significant way communicates several important things.

He trusts Barb.

He believes that she can make significant contributions to his world.

He views his wife as a partner in his work.

He wants his wife to be connected to his world.

He wants the other women at the office to see how involved he is with his spouse.

He believes that she has much to offer him.

Many men are overprotective of their workplace, and they would just as soon their wives stayed away. Work is work and home is home, and never the two should meet. This unhealthy attitude builds barriers between a husband and a wife and makes her feel that he views his world as much more important than hers.

Putting Principles into Practice

The applications of this chapter have to do with men recognizing the worth of their wives, no matter what their role in life is.

Whether she is a working career woman or a homemaker, there are things husbands can do to enhance her worth.

This is an assignment for husbands:

1. **Try the yellow-pad approach:** If for some reason your wife was permanently taken out of your life tomorrow, what are all the things you would miss about her? Make a detailed list and write it down on a yellow pad.

2. **Take a Proverbs 31 inventory:** Read carefully through Proverbs 31, and write down a list of all the valuable traits of the woman described. It would be especially helpful to read through the "paraphrase" found in this chapter and circle the qualities you see in your wife. Then, share with her those good qualities you see in her, "praising her" by thanking her for the initiative she takes in meeting your and the kids' needs in those areas.

3. **Bring your wife into your life:** How much is your spouse involved in knowing about your world? Do you communicate that it is too complex for her to understand? Take the time and energy to let her in.

> ## Highest Value and Worth
>
> The "wife of noble character" is said to be rare indeed! She is of highest value and worth, and her husband totally trusts her, not second-guessing her, but rather relying upon her, knowing her work will bring him good, not harm, **all the days of her life.**
>
> *A Proverbs 31 paraphrase*

4. **Discover her personal goals:** Talk to your wife about her long-range goals. Do you even know what her private aspirations are? Many husbands have no clue what the secret dreams of their wives are. If she has worth to you, then take the time to draw those dreams out of her.

5. **Help her dreams happen:** Most women have dreams of being more than they are and doing something special with their lives. Help your wife reach those dreams by taking a submissive approach to her needs, in this case you as the man submitting to her in the spirit of Ephesians 5:21: "Submit to one another out of reverence for Christ." Give up some of your personal goals and pursuits to be sure she has time and resources to pursue her goals.

Chapter

8

Provide Spiritual Direction

Offer Your Family Spiritual Leadership

Men are intended to provide spiritual leadership in the home, but it seems to fall more naturally on the wives and mothers, who often are more directly involved in the day to day lives of the children.

There are logical reasons why it is hard for men to assert spiritual leadership on the home front.

The worst thing a wife can do is to chide or prod her husband to be more of a spiritual leader in the home. She needs to help him in other, supportive ways.

8 Provide Spiritual Direction
Offer Your Family Spiritual Leadership

N ot long ago we attended the funeral of a spiritual giant, who had passed away after a long and fruitful life of ministry. As one tribute after another was given to this man of God, the topic of his early spiritual formation was repeated over and over. You guessed it; it was his mother who had the most powerful influence on his life in his tender, growing-up years. When you hear story after story like this, you can't help but ask yourself, "Where was Dad?" Is he some kind of an absent jerk who just doesn't care about spiritual things related to his children? Or are the issues deeper? Why is it that so often Mom is left to handle the spiritual stuff for the family?

How many times have I let Donna take the spiritual lead in our home, because I come home exhausted or I have been away on a business trip and have nothing to give? Since she just seems to be more available and conscious of their spiritual needs, she often takes the lead by default. I know it is not ideal, but sometimes I just don't have the energy to do what I should.

Thank God for Moms and Grandmothers

Several years ago we watched an in-depth interview by David Frost of Billy Graham on public television. It was an unusual interview because Billy Graham allowed David Frost to ask anything he wanted, no holds barred, for an intensive and thorough two-hour interview. Among the comments that had the most profound effect on us as we listened were his comments about the spiritual impact he had on his children. David Frost asked Billy Graham what he regretted the most as he looked back over his life. Without hesitation, Dr. Graham commented that his deepest regret was that he had not spent more time with his children. He spoke of the godliness of Ruth Graham, who had raised the children while Billy was out reaching the world through his evangelistic crusades. No one would fault Billy Graham for the marvelous work he has done, but it was a moving reminder to hear him look back on his life and regret that he had not been more active in the spiritual upbringing of his children.

How many people do you know who attribute their spiritual upbringing to a godly mother or grandmother? We have known many. It is the pattern, but it is not ideal. Actually this common approach of husbands undermines the spiritual moorings of children, who need strong signals of spiritual leadership from their dads. The father's spiritual input is crucial for the development of children. But it is the mothers who tend to be more involved in raising the children and can end up filling the vacuum of spiritual leadership. This seems to hold true of working mothers as well as the stay-at-home moms.

When it comes to spiritual tributes given by children to their parents, it seems that nine times out of ten it is Mom who gets the adulation. If a person has grown up in a Christian home and you ask that person who had the greatest spiritual influence on him or her, isn't it amazing how often that person refers back to his or her mother? For a number of important reasons, which we will explore in this chapter, moms seem to be the ones who end up having the most spiritual input in the lives of the children during their formative years.

The Best of Intentions

I consider myself to be an average spiritual father. In fact, I've been to Bible college and seminary, and perhaps might be considered by many to have "above average" spiritual potency.

And, of course, I am totally committed to the nurture and admonition of my children in the things of the Lord. However, our family often is caught by the same trap into which so many other Christian homes fall—where it seems as if Mom has the most spiritual impact on the children. How do I know? Just ask our four children—Mark, Jeremy, Andrew, and Cambria.

If you were to ask our children why they believe what they do, how they have formulated their spiritual outlook on life in terms of who has influenced them the

> **Top 10 Tip**
>
> *Seize the moment!*
>
> Make the time, and tune into those teachable moments with your kids. Share your heart! Be sure you tell your kids your Christian testimony, and explain why you choose to do what you do (go to church, not go certain places, etc.). Be sure to pray together with your kids about their problems, or particularly tough situations. And ask them to pray for you for specific needs or requests you have as well.

most, and where they get their spiritual data, I have no question in my mind that they would say they got it from their mom. I want to be a strong spiritual leader in our home, but there are a number of practical reasons that seem to fight against it.

You know things get bad when your young son goes digging through the cabinet, pulls out the family devotional Bible, and brings it to you saying, "Dad, could we please read another story tonight?" Talk about being put in my place! Confession is good for the soul, and thus I offer you this in the spirit of transparency.

The reality is that by the time I have put in my day of work, I still have the stress of making my way home, and then dealing with all of the things related to our house, yard, mail, and bills. Then there is the dinnertime, clean up, and helping with homework. By the time we get the kids off to bed, I am exhausted. There are those things that I know I should do, but they often wage war against that which I have the energy to do. What I should do is read books to them, tell them stories, pray with them, and have in-depth conversations discovering how their day went. It's not that I never do these things, but just not often enough.

With our four children you can imagine that it can take quite awhile going from room to room and child to child through that long process of getting them settled in for the evening. Walking through the house and touching base with all of them in their rooms is tough when it's tacked onto the end of a long day. It would really be nice to also have a few moments with Donna to try to keep that relationship nurtured and alive. You know, a man can also often feel that he has little or no time to himself.

Mature Christian fathers know that they should be the spiritual leaders in their home. I know that, and my counterparts know that. But in reality, so many things fight against the best of intentions. We realize that some of you women who read this are thinking, "I feel the same pressure all day: what are they whining about?" Remember we're focusing on the realities of why husbands don't engage more in spiritual leadership in the home. So bear with me. Some of the big reasons are:

Why Many Husbands Don't Engage in Spiritual Leadership in the Home:

Fatigue: Never underestimate the fatigue factor. We leave for work early in the morning, put in a hard day slugging it out at the office, pouring our energy into our life's work, and usually come home tired and ready for some relaxation. The best word that I can find to describe my feelings when I get home in the evening is "disengagement." I am engaged all day aggressively pursuing my work, and so I just want to have some downtime to do nothing. I never live the "My Three Sons" type of evening with slippers, the easy chair, and the evening paper. But I would be dishonest if I said I wouldn't love it once in a while.

Distraction: Another thing that is difficult for a working man to do is to change gears from what he has been consumed with all day at his workplace, to the issues that are raging about on the home front. It is hard to turn off the things that you thought about all day, and to turn on family life when you walk through the door at

The Protectors of Home

"God put a father in the home to be the protector of that home, to shield his wife and children from destructive influences. What we as fathers allow to come into our homes will either have a positive or negative effect on our families. God wants a father to be very sensitive to this so that the atmosphere of his home is conducive to raising children who love Christ and desire to follow Him."

From Jim Logan's *Reclaiming Surrendered Ground* (Chicago: Moody Press, 1995).

home. Years ago I had a professor in seminary who mentioned that every day when he went home from teaching, he had tried to leave his troubles at the roadside by a certain bridge that he passed on his way home. He would throw his troubles over the bridge and pick them up on his way back to work the next morning. It is a good device that illustrates what we should try to do—shift gears from the distraction of work to the needs of our spouse and children at home. But the fact of the matter is, it is difficult to make that shift . . . to throw over the load.

Despair: As Erma Bombeck said, "Guilt is the gift that keeps on giving." Many of us dads feel downright guilty and despondent by our lack of spiritual leadership in the home. You don't have to tell us that we're not doing what we should do . . . we know it all too well. And the worst thing a wife can do is to chide or prod her husband to be more of a spiritual leader in the home. She needs to help him in other ways we will get to in a moment. When I talk to fellow fathers, there seems to be the common feeling among most of them that they are failures at doing all that they should do to be the spiritual leaders in their homes. A despair can set in that makes you give up even trying.

Inadequacy: Along with feelings of despair is the complementary sense of inadequacy. Most of us don't feel that we are all that spiritually tuned up to be the great devotion leader, prayer warrior, and spiritual giant in the home. We have our own struggles, and after the hard day at work, we simply find little or no reserve from which to draw spiritual strength for our family. At times I ask my children to take the lead in family devotions, and they love it!

Absence: For many dads, they are just downright absent when Mom is not. As was the case with Billy Graham, while he wanted to be a strong influence in his home and to be a spiritual leader, he was just away from home too much to be that for his children. As Donna and I have said, in my line of work I travel often and will be away for days at a time. So Donna is often left at home to be the one who is there on a regular basis, day in and day out, to care for the needs of the children. She is the one who is there to consistently understand their needs, to pray for them, and to talk with them when spiritual issues come up. When I do return home from a trip, it can take me several days to get acclimated to family life. It is impossible for me to immediately pick up a role of leadership the moment I walk in the door. In fact, that itself is a cause of friction between us, as Donna is ready for me to get home so that she can be relieved of the total weight of family responsibility.

Fathers as Spiritual Leaders

So where do we get the idea anyway that it is up to the dads to be the spiritual leaders in the home? We begin in Scripture with the whole foundation of the Old Testament and the Jewish home, where the father was actually the teacher of the children. Public school and classroom outside of the home is actually a modern invention. Historically the parents, and particularly the fathers, were very much involved in training the children to prepare them for life.

Of course, the classic New Testament verse is found in Ephesians 6:4, where we read, "Fathers, do not exasperate your children; instead, bring them up in the training and instruction of the Lord." When Paul wrote these words to fathers, he no doubt had the Old Testament in view as a backdrop to this admonition. Paul states very clearly that it is the father's responsibility to bring up his children in the "training and instruction of the Lord." *The Bible Knowledge Commentary* magnifies the meaning of verse 4: "Fathers are addressed because they represent the governmental head of the family on whom rests the responsibility of child discipline." The commentary goes on to explain that the meaning of "do not exasperate" is "do not provoke to anger." This can be done to our children by "unreasonable demands, petty rules, or favoritism. Such actions cause children to become discouraged." Then the passage goes on: "Instead, fathers are to bring them up, that is, rear or nourish them ('provide for physical and spiritual needs') in the training ('child discipline,' including directing and correcting; 'training in righteousness' and God's 'discipline' of believers) and instruction of the Lord" (*The Bible Knowledge Commentary*, Walvoord/Zuck, p. 642).

Men, we need to take very seriously our role as protector of our home in the spiritual realm as well! Are you using biblical discernment in what movies, magazines, and other influences you are exposing yourself to? Are you doing the same with your family in the choices you allow them to make in music, video games, the Internet, and other activities? Jim Logan, an excellent family counselor, gives powerful warning to dads about this issue in his book, *Reclaiming Surrendered Ground.*

First, Logan points the finger squarely at Dad: "God put a father in the home to be the protector of that home, to shield his wife and children from destructive influences. What we as fathers allow to come into our homes will either have a positive or negative effect on our families. God wants a father to be very sensitive to this so that the atmosphere of his home is conducive to raising children who love Christ and desire to follow Him." Jesus spoke of this principle when he said, "In fact, no one can enter a strong man's house and carry off his possessions unless he first ties up the strong man. Then he can rob his house" (Mark 3:27).

In Jim Logan's work with many troubled teens, he has found that "In order to spoil a home, Satan has to attack and bind the father, the 'strong man,' and then go after his family." So when he is counseling a troubled child or teen, he first must find out what shape the father's spiritual life is in! Therefore, be sure your own life and mind are pure and right with God. Live and lead your home by the power and love of the Holy Spirit (Gal. 5:19-26). Jim also points out that a child may still choose to willfully rebel against a godly father and mother because of his or her own free will, but the principle is nevertheless crucial and valuable to practice (*Reclaiming Surrendered Ground,* Jim Logan, pp. 121-22).

Let's take a moment to look at some Old Testament admonitions for the father to be involved in the spiritual upbringing of his children:

Fathers Are to Bring Up Their Children Spiritually:

Father Abraham: God Himself said to Abraham, "For I have chosen him, so that he will direct his children and his household after him to keep the way of the Lord by doing what is right and just, so that the Lord will bring about for Abraham what he has promised him" (Gen. 18:19). We see a direct cause-effect relationship between Abraham's responsibility in directing his children and household to keep the way of the Lord, and the resultant blessing and promise that the Lord had given to Abraham and his descendants. This promised blessing is a gift we give our children (and grandchildren) as we live godly lives and train our children in godliness! Psalm 103:17—"But from everlasting to everlasting the Lord's love is with those who fear him, and his righteousness with their children's children."

Ten Commandments: In accordance with the Ten Commandments, the guarantee that generations to follow would love the Lord their God was dependent upon the fathers' passing down to their children an understanding and a love for the law of God. Deuteronomy 6:6-7: "These commandments that I give you today are to be upon your hearts. Impress them on your children. Talk about them when you sit at home and when you walk along the road, when you lie down and when you get up." It is clear from the context that this admonition goes directly to the elders and fathers of Israel.

Solomon's wisdom: Finally, in the classic text from the Book of Proverbs, which were the words of wisdom of Solomon to the fathers of Israel, we find: "Train a child in the way he should go, and when he is old he will not turn from it" (Prov. 22:6). What could be more obvious than this admonition for a father to be actively involved in the process of training the child in the ways of God?

So our #8 way to love your wife is to provide spiritual direction. Take the initiative to talk to your kids about your own spiritual journey. It's just not fair to your wife and to your children's mother to have her carry the spiritual ball in your home. It is also not fair to the kids to expect Mom to be the spiritual anchor in your home. There are dangers of relying strictly upon Mom to handle the spiritual stuff.

The Dangers of Leaving It All to Mom

- Kids won't have a strong example of God as their Heavenly Father.

- Dad neglecting his God-given responsibility, with many negative results in family choices and stability.

- Putting too much pressure on Mom, which God never intended.

- Providing a bad example for sons and daughters who will grow up one day to be parents themselves.

Hero Husbands We Know

I (Donna) look back on my childhood with great joy and some awe at my parents. My father was a busy pastor. In the first thirteen years of my life, our church grew from a group of 50 to over 600 members. My mom, also involved in music and ministry as a pastor's wife, was a full-time homemaker. She carried much of the weight of raising three daughters. She knew how to let go, though. She instinctively knew the importance of allowing her girls to be very close to their daddy. We all were. Although each of us felt unconditionally loved and treasured by our dad, we all knew that he loved us equally.

The close relationship we had with him started when we were very young. I remember the story my parents would tell of the time when my older sister, Rhonda, was a "tow-headed" toddler. Dad was closed away in a room at the front of our house and deep in study for his sermon. Rhonda was busy playing, but she kept trying to interrupt Daddy to try to get him to play with her. With some frustration, he tried to tell her he must be left alone to work. With her simple "baby-talk" words, Rhonda said, "I just want to be with you, Daddy." Wisely, Dad set aside his work for a short time to take Rhonda in his arms and "be with her" for just a few minutes. That was all she needed, and she was off, blonde curls bouncing behind her.

Unlike so many other pastor's kids, or "PKs" for short, we all grew up loving the ministry. We all loved our church and felt a part of what our parents were doing. We truly were at the church, which was adjacent to our home, every time the doors were opened. Our church *was* home. We *loved* it, and all of the people were our extended family.

We usually had devotions after supper as a family. Dad would read a Bible story and ask us questions to see how well we had listened. Then we would pray together. Our home was always open to others. We had visiting missionaries, families, and those in need in our home on a weekly basis. Dad and Mom lived the same whether visitors were there or not. The Lord was the center of our lives, and serving Him was the outpouring of our love for Him. No artificial "because *you* are the pastor's kids" laws were laid on us. Any rules or behavior expectations were always well explained (and demonstrated to us). The bottom line was always that we are believers, and our lives belong to the Lord. *He* is the reason for all of our choices and actions.

Much of my dad's spiritual leadership to us occurred in the natural daily happenings of our lives. He was very strong in disciplining us! It was, however, *always* tempered by his unshakable love and acceptance of us. We knew the boundaries, and Dad was always extra creative in discipline if we overstepped a boundary in relationship to honoring the Lord. The most painful and powerful one I remember was when I was about ten or eleven.

My sister, Rhonda, and cousin, Jan, were both older than I. Since our home, the church parsonage, was right next door to our church, we would often go over to the church gym to play or ride bikes around all of the sidewalks. One sunny afternoon, we were in the church sanctuary "hopping" pews! It was great fun, racing from pew to pew using the pews as hurdles. But then

Dad walked in. Boy, were we in trouble!

Our punishment for such wanton disregard for the holiness of our place of worship was to have us pull all of the weeds bordering our whole church parking lot the rest of that summer day. Each of us was given a section to pull. Since we had to show our own pile to him, we spent the day basically alone with our thoughts and worked far away from one another. Never again did any of us consider misusing our place of worship.

As we grew into our teen years, our relationship with our dad became even more important. I respect my mom so much for having the wisdom and maturity to let us be closer to our dad than we were to her at times. Those early foundational years of his spiritual leadership and open relationship were key. We had *always* known that no matter how busy Dad was, we came first. Our weekly family nights and yearly vacations also gave us time to build a strong relationship with our parents.

On Our Image of God Coming from Our Earthly Fathers

"Recently, I heard a wonderful message where the speaker asked us all to do something unusual. He asked us to picture in our minds the Lord's arms. He illustrated many ways we might picture them. Many would picture them closed in front in a position of retribution or disapproval. Some would picture them open in a welcoming way. My immediate picture to my surprise was of my own father's arms enfolded around me in a loving, safe, accepting, secure embrace."

—*Donna's reflection on her father*

The security we felt in our father's love and openness of sharing carried over into the rocky teen years. When I struggled with a relationship with a boyfriend and the temptations thrown at any teenager, I could talk to Dad. Unlike most of my friends, I didn't have the desire or need to turn to cigarettes, beer, marijuana, or sex to find happiness. When I was feeling down, I knew I could turn to my parents and to the Lord, who gave me all I needed. My friends were dumfounded! Why not just *one* puff? Why not just *one* drink? It was obvious they did it to feel a high, to feel better . . . but I felt just *great* without it.

Yet even in those times when I would be in a period of rebellion, Dad did it right. Sometimes he'd just say a simple, "Gettin' kinda' cocky, young lady." Coming from him, those words would cut through quickly. But more often, Dad would just take the situation to God in prayer. Neither he nor Mom would say anything to me directly. Inevitably, the Lord would use other people or reading to convict me of my rebellious spirit. After confessing to God, I'd always go to tell my parents and ask their forgiveness too. I remember being so shocked that not only had they known of my rebellion, but they had *trusted God* enough to leave me in His hands.

Recently, I heard a wonderful message where the speaker asked us all to do something unusual. He asked us to picture in our minds the Lord's arms. He illustrated many ways we might picture them. Many would picture them closed in front in a position of retribution or disapproval. Some would picture them open in a welcoming way. My immediate picture to my surprise was of my *own father's arms* enfolded around me in a loving, accepting, safe and secure embrace. Wow! That's certainly a beautiful example of spiritual leadership that *works*. Though not perfect, it created in me an image of our Lord as my own

Heavenly Father who loves *me* . . . like my father's arms, but even more so!"

First, from the example of my own father, here are some hints on how to be a good spiritual leader in your home:

How to Improve Your Leadership in the Home:

1. **Pray!** Above all, my dad is a man of prayer. He and Mom prayed for each of us and our future mates, even before our births. Every problem was prayed about, every need brought to God.

2. **Listen!** From the time your children are young, make time to give them your undivided attention. This should be on a regular basis so they feel you truly care. I still treasure the breakfasts out with Daddy I had with him alone, and I continue to enjoy those rare occasions we can be together.

3. **Put your family first.** Learn how to set aside your work— leave it at the office, and build a relationship with them. That will establish important memories for each child.

4. **Love them unconditionally.** Encourage your children to be who God wants them to be. Ask the Lord to show you the special needs of each child, and then be creative in leading them to grow.

5. **Live what you believe.** That does not mean you have to be perfect. Just be willing to walk according to God's Word, and *ask* forgiveness from your kids or wife if you blow it by your words or actions. Then start over again.

6. **Seize the moment.** Make the time, and tune into those teachable moments with your kids. Share your heart. Be sure you tell your kids your own spiritual journey, and explain why you choose to do what you do (go to church, not go certain places, etc.). Be sure to pray together with your kids about their problem or situation. And ask them to pray for you, giving specific needs or requests you have as well.

7. **Take time *alone* with each child to focus on him or her.** Talk through with your spouse each of your visions of the needs and gifts of each child, and get alone with each one on a regular basis. Hans schedules one or two of his trips a year to include one of our children. He has taken each of them to various places around the world, spending focused time alone with them.

We don't claim to have mastered the male spiritual leadership issue in our home. However, Donna and I have worked together to provide solutions so that we can attempt to raise our children in the right atmosphere. Some of the other practices that we follow, which we would pass on to you for your consideration, are:

Relief Tips for Guilty Fathers:

- Lower your expectations and do what you can do.
- Think bite-size pieces: start with having family devotions, maybe just once or twice a week. Use a creative devotional book to help you, and pray together. Today's Christian bookstores are filled with great family devotional aids. Then come up with a list of annual minimal goals for what you would like to do with the children to provide spiritual influence.

- Be honest with your children about your struggles, and ask them for their input. Confession is good for not only your soul, but theirs.

- Make this area a part of your accountability group.

- Beg, borrow, and steal any good ideas you can find from other fathers who seem to make this work.

- If you fail, just start over. The future is a blank check you can invest how you decide.

Support Tips for Wives and Mothers:

- Learn to back off. Work at allowing your husband the freedom and room to lead.

- Learn to back up. Pray for your husband, for the Lord to help him lead spiritually, and remember to support him when he does take the initiative.

- *When* you both fail (not *if* you fail), get back up and give it another try. Don't feel defeated. Starting over is always better than giving up.

Chapter
9

Share the Load
*Home Life Is Not
a Spectator Sport*

Husbands have a vested interest in not learning how to do things well around the house. If they do well, it might become a regular assignment! So men all across the land learn to practice what we call "intentional incompetence."

The libido of the American man is focused almost entirely upon his business so that as a husband he is glad to have no responsibilities.

A strong part of a woman's identity is expressed through her home.

In the words of one wife: "If I could change one thing about my husband: I would change his quiet spectatorship to active involvement and inquisitiveness of what's happening in my life and the children's."

9 Share the Load
Home Life Is Not a Spectator Sport

Bill Cosby has a classic video of a stage act that is perhaps a bit dated these days—it is called, "Bill Cosby, Himself," and it remains one of the staples of the Finzel family's humor collection. After renting it for years, Donna gave me my own copy for my birthday. When we really want a laugh, the kind where we have to stop the tape to catch our breath from laughing so hard, we can always count on Bill.

In one of the best routines, called "chocolate cake," Bill's wife wakes him at 6 A.M. one morning to fix the kids' breakfast (they raised five kids). Of course, Bill has no interest whatsoever in getting up at that inhumane hour. He grunts and rolls over, going back to sleep. "It is her job. Let her do it," he reasons. In the next moment she is standing over him with a bucket of ice-cold water. "If you don't get up in five seconds and get downstairs and fix them breakfast, I will soak you with this bucket of water!" she screams. All *she* wants is one morning in bed! Is that too much to ask of a father, who leaves you to get the kids up and running all other mornings?

Bill finally rolls out of bed with one eye open and goes downstairs in his robe, angrily groping around the kitchen for something to give the kids for breakfast. The first child down, his little eight-year-old daughter, spies the chocolate cake on the counter and says, "Dad, can I have chocolate cake for breakfast?" Of *all the things* in the kitchen, she spotted the cake first, even though it was behind him on the counter! "She's got x-ray vision!" Bill begins to think, "Well, actually what is in chocolate cake? milk, eggs, butter, flour. Sure, why not? Those are, after all, the ingredients of a balanced breakfast." Pretty soon all the children are in the kitchen, and Dad is serving up chocolate cake for everyone for breakfast. As he serves, the children sing in blissful tune, *"Dad is great—he gave us the chocolate cake! Dad is great— he gave us the chocolate cake!"*

Things are going great until . . . you guessed it. Mom comes downstairs. Everything falls silent—the party is over. She spots the kids and the chocolate cake. Of course, they turn on Dad: "He made us eat it, Mom!" With fire in her eyes she tells him *to go back to bed*—she will have to feed the kids breakfast herself if she wants it done right. And instead of a problem, Bill scores a success. *Back to bed*—that is what he wanted all along! He can hardly keep the smile on the inside as he charges back up the stairs to their bedroom.

Husbands have a vested interest in not learning how to do things well around the house. If they do it well, it might become a regular assignment! So men all across the land learn to practice what we call "intentional incompetence." The more proficient a man gets at a domestic duty, the more he will be relied on to perform it as a regular chore. As wrong as it might seem, many men just don't want to walk down that road. This intentional incompetence is really a form of subconscious denial.

Agree or Disagree?
One way to look at it

"The libido of the American man is focused almost entirely upon his business, so that as a husband he is glad to have no responsibilities. . . . It is what I call the laziness of the American man."

—Carl Jung, as quoted in *Woman,* by Charles Swindoll

Comedienne Diane Ford put it best: A woman works her tail off all the time. The guy does two things around the house, and he's got to show her, "Honey, look! I fixed the screen! And look over there: I washed my dish! I picked my shirt up!" What can the wife say? "Well, why don't we put a little star on the refrigerator?"

One complaint we hear over and over again is wives having to wait on their husbands to fix things around the house. The husband says he will do it (read *promises*), but then neglects to ever get to it. If the wife takes the matter into her own hands, she gets chewed out for (a) not letting him do it, or (b) spending "our good money" to have someone else do it.

One Couple's Experience:

> **She** (at the bedside table, stacked high with books yet to be read): Honey, I think I'm going to go out today and get a bookcase for all this stuff. Want to come?
>
> **He:** Come? No . . . gee . . . I've got too much to do today. Besides, why spend the money when I can make one myself? How about if I take next Saturday and get some wood and build one. Can it wait until then?
>
> **She:** Well, sure. . . .
>
> [Cut to next Saturday, A.M.]
>
> **She:** So, you're gonna' make that bookcase today?
>
> **He:** Don't bug me. I said I'd get to it . . . soon.

Months go by. No bookcase gets built. Finally in frustration she goes out and buys the bookcase. You know what his response will be: He gets *really* mad: "What'd you do that for?" he asks. "I told you I'd take care of it."

One wife was so fed up with her husband not picking up after himself that she tried a new approach. Nagging never worked and only annoyed him. "On our anniversary, I gave Chris a card that listed all the wonderful things he was to me—what a great cook he was, how much I admired his patience with the kids, and that I thought he still had the most beautiful blue eyes. At the bottom in really small print, I wrote: "If you could only learn to pick up after yourself, you'd be perfect."

"He laughed when he read it and said, 'I didn't realize . . . Does my sloppiness really upset you that much?' Can you believe it? Where had he been for the last ten arguments? But he got better after that. And now when he leaves his junk around, I only have to point to it and he gets the message." (*Good Housekeeping,* March 1996, "Your Husband's Bad Habits," by Sara Nelson, pp. 80-81.)

Her Home Is Her Identity

A strong part of a woman's identity is expressed through her home. Whether she is consciously aware of it or not, we believe it is true. Her home says to the world, "This is who I am, and here is what I'm like." Considering some *women* are unaware of how strongly their identity is tied to their homes, it should not be surprising that *men* are completely baffled by this fact. They say the common, "Oh, you care too much what people think," when they see their wives' seemingly excessive effort to care for the home. Hans will ask if we can have someone over for dinner at the drop of a hat and then get upset when I go into the "get the house ready" mode. He'll say something like, "What's wrong with them seeing how we live in the natural?" Men!

To be fair, some of us truly do get obsessive about our homes "when company is coming." We need to step back and remember our priority of people (including our husbands and kids) above tasks. But men also need to look beyond their gut feeling that their wives demand too much when it comes to the home and what they want out of their hus-

This Is Who I Am

A strong part of a woman's identity is expressed through her home. Whether she is consciously aware of it or not, I believe it is true. Her home says to the world, "This is who I am, and here is what I'm like."

bands. They must see how much of a woman's identity is wrapped up in her home and how she sees the home as an external expression of her own inner self. Because of that, an important way he can love his wife is to refuse to be a spectator. Out of love for her, he should choose to jump in, taking initiative with household responsibilities.

There are innumerable varieties of homes, each reflecting the unique woman and family members who live there. Our homes display both our strengths and our weaknesses. Some women are, of course, messier by nature. Their personality is more laid back—they don't even see the mess. Many of these women are super mothers, who are great with crafts and doing other creative activities with their kids. Being like that is, of course, a valid expression of who they are. "Life is messy" as the saying goes. Life is also short, and spending time with our husbands and kids should take priority over a perfect home.

Pity the poor family who lives the other extreme—what I call a "maniac perfectionist" who drives herself and everyone around her crazy with her demands for cleanliness. We all well know that there is absolutely no end to the work of homemaking. Thus a balance must be found to have a truly happy home for all. We women do need to remember Scripture commands us to be "given to hospitality." If we insist upon everything being perfect, we won't have an open home. After all, "cleanliness is next to godliness" is nowhere in the Bible. Even when it's not "finished" in our minds, or as clean as we'd necessarily like, we must make it an open place to share the love of Christ with others. Real life happens here. Our kids' friends, neighbors, the hurting—they all should be coming through our doors.

The easygoing way of messy women may also be a thorn in their husband's side. The Bible warns against laziness and the results of being a sluggard; some women do struggle with this. If you struggle with this, ask the Lord to help you with His fruit of self-control. Then seek out advice and good books on organization and discipline.

Top 10 Tip

A Cry from One Young Mother

If I could change one thing about my husband: "I would change his quiet spectatorship to active involvement and inquisitiveness of what's happening in my life and the children's."

Finally, there are also those who struggle with depression, with physical limitations, or the overwhelming demands of many young children. This would include women with demanding jobs outside the home. These women may be unable to keep their homes as they would like. They need even more the attention of their husbands in carrying a greater weight in household work.

Just Do It

This chapter probably wouldn't have made our "Top Ten" except for how strongly this issue of men's passivity came through to us from those wives who completed our survey. These women are very frustrated and feel stuck between a "rock and a hard place" on this issue of husbands doing their part at home.

Listen to this cry from a young mother on the East Coast. In response to our question, *"If you could change anything about your husband, what would it be?"* she actually made a list for her husband:

1. Change "I love you" statements to actions of love: Help with the dishes, pray with the kids at night, and work with the children to make them do their chores and have quiet times each day.

2. Change your laziness and TV watching to help with the homework and reading books to the children in the evenings.

3. Change your view that our two separate roles in life don't meet anywhere. You come home each evening with this attitude—"I work all day, and I'm tired at night, and I'm going to relax."

4. Change quiet spectatorship to active involvement and inquisitiveness of what's happening in my life and the children's.

Our hearts go out to this friend. She doesn't have the courage to give him this list, and that might not be the right approach anyway. On top of these attitudes that she has to live with, *she home schools their three children,* and a fourth child is on the way! What options does this wife have? Really, with little support from her husband, there are only two that seem obvious. The two common options seem to be:

Option one: End up being a "nag" because jobs don't get taken care of. Friction grows.

Option two: Forget about it and try to ignore those things that are left undone. Resentment builds.

Obviously neither option is good. Proverbs warns over and over again of the damage nagging can do to the family. We believe that nagging creates quarrels nine times out of ten, as seen clearly in these verses. Here are a few powerful admonitions from the Book of Proverbs:

"A quarrelsome wife is like a constant dripping"—Proverbs 19:13.

"Better to live on a corner of the roof than share a house with a quarrelsome wife"—Proverbs 21:9.

"Better to live in a desert than with a quarrelsome and ill-tempered wife"—Proverbs 21:19.

We women must be careful not to allow nagging to be a characteristic of our lives. But husbands, you should also be reminded that wealth doesn't bring peace into your home. Too many men are workaholics, falling into the trap of believing that providing plenty of money will fix anything. Financial well-being is not what your family needs or wants most from you. You need to engage yourself—to carry your share to enjoy a joyful home with a happy family.

"Better a dry crust with peace and quiet than a house full of feasting, with strife"—Proverbs 17:1.

Another way women deal with passive husbands is to "forget about it." This doesn't work either. Some women give up and decide not to let their frustration control them. But neglect on the part of the husband of those household involvements and problems is actually neglect of her. Men, as we already said, realize that your home reflects your wife. She usually cares more than you do that those things get done. Loving her is meeting her needs. Although she may be able to forget it for a time, it's possible she may only be stuffing it.

There are several other options for this couple struggling with the husband's responsibilities. One is for the wife to pray for her husband to change. Ask God to bring some men into his life who can be a positive example to him. Pray that he will get involved in your church with a men's small group. Another option would be for the two of you to get some professional counseling. The couple in our story here is headed for trouble, and one of the best things they can do at this stage in their life together is to talk to their pastor or a counselor about their problems.

Money Can't Buy You Love

Many men get hung up on the notion that money is the solution to all the family's problems. If they just work harder to bring home more money, then she will be more happy. I am certain that for most of the women I know, they would rather have more of their husbands' personal attention and involvement at home than more money in the checking account.

The marriage vows we repeated years ago said, "In sickness and in health, for richer or poorer." We have been in many levels of financial security in our years of marriage. As newlyweds, we struggled to make ends meet. Next, we had some childless years with two incomes in California when we had lots of freedom financially. Then we spent ten years living overseas in Austria on a limited income and the added expenses of four children that came along in those years. We have moved many times, adapting to many varied homes and income levels, working together to make a happy home.

Our point here is that no matter what your financial resources are (or are not), you can make a house a home. You can give your wife that place of joy to express herself. Join her willingly no matter your circumstances by being involved. By choosing to step up to the plate at home, and getting out of the stands, you'll enjoy a whole new level of closeness.

Moving twelve times in our twenty-five years of marriage certainly was not our plan, and is not ideal, but in spite of all that stress and work, we had fun! Much of the joy I feel as I look back on all of those places we lived comes from our working together as equal partners to make each one into our Finzel home.

In our own life, it means so much to me that Hans cares enough about me to help "make it happen" in our home. This would include hiring outside help for some jobs. Whatever needs doing such as wallpapering, putting in extra outlets in a kitchen, or even heavier jobs, I'm very blessed that one of the most natural ways Hans expresses his love for me is in this way.

Hero Husbands We Know

Donna and I have the rare and valuable privilege of both being from families where the mother and father stayed together their whole married lives in a positive and nurturing marriage. In Chapter Eight you heard about Donna's dad and his spiritual leadership in the home. He and Mom Bubeck have been married over fifty years, and their relationship is truly a tribute to doing it right.

I grew up in a very different home than Donna did, being a first-generation American living in the home of immigrants from Germany. My parents moved to America right after World War II to work for the U.S. government in building missiles in the budding space program. My father's boss was Dr. Wernher von Braun, and he and a group of scientists and engineers were brought to America after World War II to begin the U.S. space program. My family, along with 100 other German families, immigrated to and settled in Huntsville, Alabama, on the southern rim of the beautiful Smoky Mountains.

Our home was a traditional German home, where we spoke the language of our parents. My experience was typical of a third-culture kid, in many ways similar to the lives of expatriate children growing up in foreign cultures. It was a good childhood, and to this day I believe I model my own role as husband and father based upon the example of my dad even more than I realize it.

My dad, whom we called "Vati"—German for "daddy"—was certainly not a perfect man. The older I get the more I realize that some of my own inadequacies are the same inadequacies that I saw in him. The awesome power of genetics! One thing my dad was great in was being involved in the home as a helping father and husband to my mom. My dad had an intense career in the U.S. space program. You can imagine the pressure during the years when they were building rockets to put us on the moon. I remember hearing the roaring blast of rocket engines being tested at the NASA space center in Huntsville, even though the test stands were twenty miles from our home!

After the Apollo program came the space shuttle, and there was always plenty to do with long intense hours of work. And yet I could always tell that my father loved his family more than he loved his work. I also noticed through the years how much he loved being alone with my mom as they would take trips together to different places around the world. They loved traveling together more than any other recreational experience.

When my father was home, he was really home. He didn't have hobbies or lots of personal friends who took him away from home when he wasn't working. He was busily engaged in the evenings and every weekend, taking care of the house and making it a home. I remember his Saturday morning trips to the hardware store to gather the necessary equipment for that weekend's "honey do" list. He took good care of everything that broke down in the home, and he did it quickly and proficiently. I can also remember the countless hours he spent working with me on my go-carts and then later numerous collections of motorcycles, which I acquired as a teenager. He was there for me, and he was engaged in my life when I needed him.

Unfortunately, my father was a smoker, and he died of lung cancer in 1984. My mother never remarried because as far as she was concerned, there could never be a man who would ever closely measure up to the stature of my father. To this day she worships him and, of course, misses him intensely. Vati taught me a lot of great values. He showed me how to be a good husband and father who engages in the things that need to be done around the house to keep the family corporation operational. He wasn't perfect, and I'm not perfect. But I do thank him for providing such a strong example in this important area of husbandhood.

Putting Principles into Practice

This chapter is one that could easily be seen as a put-down on men. Women hate to nag their husbands, but the alternatives are none the more appealing. Husbands working in the home is an area that many men don't want to hear about, but it's an issue that is very real and on the front burner for most wives.

What's a husband and father to do? In two words, "focused engagement." We like the way our friend on the East Coast puts it: *Change quiet spectatorship to active involvement and inquisitiveness of what's happening in my life and the children's.* A few other tips to help you along your way:

Developing Focused Engagement

1. **Remember her view of your home**—everything about your home matters to your wife because it reflects her. Part of respecting and loving her is to understand how important this is to her.

2. **Don't procrastinate**—whatever that means in your life, whether you set a time limit to do what she asks for fix-it jobs or "do it now" in the case of taking the garbage out or other small requests.

3. **Do some research by asking her**—What needs to be done that I could do tonight? What things around the house bother you the most, and which, if completed, would mean the most to you?

4. **Set aside one Saturday a month for projects**—Many dads spend Saturdays with kids at the ball games. Why not make one Saturday a month a day for those projects she needs done around the house? Or take a vacation day just to catch up with chores around the house. Getting down and dirty with power tools is great therapy and a good change of pace for many men.

5. **If you're not going to do it soon—then let it go!** Back her up when she hires someone else to do it. As in the case of the wife with the bookshelf or the woman who wanted to pay to have someone clean the windows, don't make

promises that you can't keep. She is happy, you're off the hook, and life is good.

6. **Take some initiative**—make her day by doing tasks without being asked. Doing dishes, picking up (or telling kids to pick up) things, cleaning bathrooms, and so on are not exclusively *her* job description. You are not "helping" her; you are doing your share of the household partnership.

Chapter

10

Give Romance a Chance

Don't Give Up on Dating After You Say "I Do"

All work and no play can make marriages a very dull place to be.

Dating in marriage is the ongoing courtship that re-wins your spouse over and over again.

Two people can have a physical relationship without ever being intimate; and conversely, two people can grow into intimacy without departing into sexuality.

The beautiful children, who are God's blessing and the very product of our love, can snuff out the flames of passion that got it all going.

10 Give Romance a Chance
Don't Give Up on Dating After You Say "I Do"

A few weeks ago we went on an overnight trip to the mountains—just the two of us. We stayed in a quaint inn with wonderful views. Even though it was a short trip, just twenty-four hours, our focused time alone went a long way to recalibrate our relationship. Talking in the car, a romantic dinner out, relaxed time to share around coffee and breakfast all blended together to refresh our relationship.

We have short dates and long dates, sometimes just a cup of coffee, often dinner out for just the two of us. Every once in a while we will farm out the kids and have a whole weekend away from the children. We love them, but face it: their mom and dad are much better parents if they keep their marriage alive. The best thing we can do for our children is to keep our marriage healthy and happy.

Not long ago our getaway was three days on a beach in Southern California. During those times I sometimes say to Donna, "Oh, yes, *now* I remember, you're that spunky girl I married twenty-five years ago!" She, more than me, has the chance in those moments to climb out of her "mother" role and back into the courtship and carefree role that sparked the romance to begin with. Dating is one of the best ways we have found to keep our marriage fresh. It gives us time to communicate, and it lets Donna know I want to be with her. We do things together that we used to do before life became so serious and full of family responsibility.

Have you ever tried to calculate how much of your communication with your spouse is about family matters, bills, problems, and broken things that need fixing? These are the surface things that consume life and often account for 99 percent of communication between husband and wife. When was the last time you had tender moments of personal talk about how each other is *doing?* Dating in marriage is the ongoing courtship to re-win your spouse over and over.

Nothing Kills Dating Like Kids Do

Life has its strange ironies. Dating leads to love and love to marriage. Marriage usually brings kids, who can stifle the intimate love that started the whole process to begin with. The dating is over—done, finished! The beautiful children, who are God's blessing and the very product of our love, can snuff out the flames that got it all going.

Life changes drastically in a marriage when children arrive. Hans and I had talked about wanting four children when we were newly married. That changed quickly after the birth of our first child, Mark.

In our early years of marriage after graduate school, we were in a ministry in Long Beach, California. Hans was on a church staff, and I worked full time for the Oilwell division of U.S. Steel. Without the responsibility of children, we shared daily and deeply about our work. Hans knew details about my work and relationships at Oilwell; I, in turn, worked side by side with him in ministry.

As we began building a ministry to young married couples, we planned retreats and getaways with our growing group of couples. Our marriage grew, and the Lord gave us the joy of helping young couples grow in maturity in their relationships with Christ and with each other. The freedom we all had, we took great advantage of, spending time as a group, going out together after church, and enjoying hours of deep fellowship. Only three couples in our group had children. They

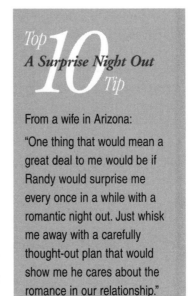

Top **10** *Tip*
A Surprise Night Out

From a wife in Arizona:

"One thing that would mean a great deal to me would be if Randy would surprise me every once in a while with a romantic night out. Just whisk me away with a carefully thought-out plan that would show me he cares about the romance in our relationship."

each had only one child. Their children tagged along, and we all enjoyed them immensely. After one of the couples had another child, we saw their involvement change. Often they wouldn't be able to go out with us. The kids were sick or had to go to bed. We didn't understand very well, but we tried to adjust, although we missed their fellowship.

We observed the change that children made in the lives of our friends, but we certainly did not comprehend the true impact until several years later when our own son arrived. As we soon came to realize, *the adjustment of having a child is much greater than the adjustment of getting married and living with another person as a mate.*

After several years of great ministry in Long Beach, we knew our heart's passion was to work in ministry overseas behind the

Iron Curtain in Europe. We applied and were accepted to work with CBInternational in the summer of 1980 as their first staff to focus on Eastern Europe. We said goodbye to our friends, ministry, and my job in the late summer of 1981, and landed in Vienna, Austria, in September 1981. I was six months pregnant with our first child.

What a shock parenthood was! For six years we had enjoyed our independence and involvement in each other's worlds. Overnight, this precious new life had turned our world upside-down!

Me? Self-Centered?

I (Donna) remember clearly that one of the most amazing realities that hit me was how this little person confronted me with the depth and power of my own self-centeredness. By his very nature as a helpless, 100 percent dependent little baby, Mark's needs forced themselves upon me. *My* own needs and desires, and those of Hans, had to come second. It was just the physical realities of caring for a newborn baby—a very physically exhausting experience. Whew!

The fact that I had never been home full time in our years of marriage magnified the shock of parenthood for me. Many women go through these two major adjustments at the same time: becoming a mother and leaving the work force. It's a double whammy on the self-confidence for sure. Added to those two adjustments were the stresses of a new culture and new language, and the reality of being a foreigner in a strange country. Then (as if the potential for depression is not enough already), a typical day of Vienna winter was what we called the "gray gloom." All this bombardment of change led to one reeling new mom.

How Bad Can It Get?

After thirty years of marriage, the wife was ready to finally throw in the towel. "I have had it living with you," she moaned in disgust. "You never tell me you love me. There is no romance left in our marriage. It has been years since I have heard those three words come out of your mouth."

In a stoic, cool manner the husband replied, "Look, I told you I loved you when we got married—if I change my mind, I'll let you know."

I remember telling other friends that now that Hans and I had met the reality of parenthood, we were no longer considering the possibility of having four kids. We said, "Maybe, just *maybe*, we'll have two!"

In Vienna, we were part of a team of people from thirteen different ministries, all working together in an organization called "BEE," or Biblical Education by Extension. Our leader was Dr. Jody Dillow. His wife, Linda, was my mentor and friend. And as the mother of three school-age children, Linda's wisdom on motherhood was my salvation on many a rough day in those early days of adjustment to my new life. One area that Linda was committed to, beyond all else, was the need for marriage to have first place in our lives. In spite of the needs and demands of our new son, she emphasized that we must put our marriage first.

Linda put her advice into action by volunteering to baby-sit Mark for us when he was only about a month old, so we could have our first postpartum date. I remember the strange feeling it was to leave Mark and go out with Hans alone. We enjoyed a wonderful couple of hours of just sharing together and focusing on each other. Of course, we talked about our precious son, but we were alone! This was a good breaking point for us, and from that time on we reestablished dating as a regular part of our married life.

That was twenty years ago, but the lessons have stuck with us. We're so grateful that at that time in our lives Linda and Jody were there for us with their admonitions. They lived the example of laying aside other responsibilities, especially parenthood, to give focused attention to their mate and marriage. We began a pattern that has proven to be the key to the growth and ongoing closeness of our marriage. We made time to be together alone. In fact, we highly recommend Linda's book that has been a great resource for wives for a couple of decades now: *Creative Counterpart* (Thomas Nelson: Nashville, 1977).

Don't Be Afraid to Leave Them Alone

By now you get the picture that we both believe dating must be a priority all through a marriage. We believe this is one of the most common and damaging failures couples make after they have children. They fail to set aside time for each other. It seems impossible to schedule, and it's hard emotionally to "let go" of parenting, even for a few hours or a night away. But couples often allow the daily reality of parenting children to take precedence over their marriage. If they do that as a lifelong pattern, there will be *no relationship left* when the kids are gone. The empty nest will also be empty of any meaningful relationship.

Men, do you know how much your wife needs to know you value her? Time alone with her, focused on her and your relationship with her, communicates mountains of love and affection to her. Even if you can't see it, *relationship* is what she needs all your married lives. It's possible your wife may have developed patterns of being unwilling to leave the kids at all. Her need for time alone with you may be buried, and she may need to be pulled away from the kids at times.

Can Children Get in the Way?

As our children started to arrive, it became more and more difficult to steal the time to maintain our closeness. We tell every young couple that is expecting their first child the same warning: *Adjusting to having a child is many times more difficult than adjusting to marriage.* The couple without a child can live a pretty self-centered life, but that first baby will knock the selfishness right out of you both. (At least we hope that the father is there to do his share.) As my (Hans') father told me upon the arrival of our first child, "Making children is easy, son. It's raising them that is the hard part."

Although we made time alone a priority, even after the kids came, both Hans and I would say for certain that the years when we had babies and young toddlers were the toughest on our marriage. Our commitment to our marriage was the same. But our closeness was not.

Here is a time of danger in a marriage. A woman's natural need for affection and closeness can in some measure be met in her children. A woman can easily use the precious gift of babies— nursing, rocking, and holding them—to try to meet that need for affection. It is normal to love and nurture her baby, but God intends for your *marriage* to be the place where this need for affection as women is met. It is not healthy for parents to seek to have those needs met through their children. Unhealthy attachments and abnormal expectations of children will result.

In view of these challenges, a few special tips for wives and husbands would be good to take note of here:

Special Tip For Women: If you are allowing the intimacy you have with your children to take first place in your emotions, time, and energy, you must take steps to change that. If you are early on in child-rearing, I would challenge you to step back and ask yourself if you are guilty of this. If so, take action. Seek wise counsel from a godly older woman, counselor, or pastor. Then make changes to put your husband first in your heart again. You may need to plan a getaway yourself (without children) and surprise your husband (see suggestions at the end of this chapter, and don't necessarily leave all the romance to your husband).

If you are further along in your child-rearing years, and this has been your pattern, you have a greater challenge! Your whole family is used to this, and certainly your husband feels like second place (or worse) in your life and time. He has probably withdrawn emotionally from you as well, and the strength of your marriage may well be crumbling, whether it's evident or not. Although patterns like these are difficult to change, change they must if your marriage is to endure and be all God intends it to be. Ask you husband some straight questions:

1 How do you feel our relationship has changed since we had children?

2 Do you feel that I put you first in my life?

3 What are 3 things I could do to "put you first" in my life?

Special Tip for Men: If you see this as the portrait of your marriage and home, you need to realize where you have failed to get involved in understanding your wife. Recognize her needs for affection, and set aside time for her! Remember how you need to study her as "the feminine one" from 1 Peter 3, learning to cherish those womanly ways that make her unique.

Building Habits for a Healthy Relationship

The issue of *relationship* is what seems to puzzle many men. They don't seem to need it, but the wife can't get enough of it. Perhaps the wisdom of Dave Barry is appropriate here to show just how differently men and women view this issue:

Tips for Women: How to Have a Relationship with a Guy

Contrary to what many women believe, it's fairly easy to develop a long-term stable, intimate and mutually fulfilling relationship with a guy. Of course, this guy has to be a Labrador retriever. With human guys, it's extremely difficult. This is because guys don't really grasp what women mean by the term *relationship*.

We're not talking about different wavelengths here. We're talking about different *planets,* in completely different *solar systems.* A woman cannot communicate meaningfully with a man about their relationship any more than she can meaningfully play chess with a duck. Because the sum total of man's thinking on this particular topic is as follows: Huh? (From *Dave Barry's Complete Guide to Guys,* Random House, 1995)

I (Hans) found out early in our marriage through trial and error just how important relationship was to Donna. If I was going to express my love to her, it meant making time every day for our relationship. After our wedding we settled into life together in Dallas, Texas where I was finishing my master's degree. Though the studies were tough, I made the decision early on in our marriage that I would always go to bed with Donna when it was time for lights out. In fact, in those early years, I remember how comfy-cozy it was that we could actually go to sleep with our toes touching. A good-night kiss might seem like something simple, but it is a strong statement of the intimacy of a marriage as the years go on.

That little habit became a lifelong commitment: to always go to bed together each night. One wife wrote us about a practice her husband has that greatly frustrates her in this arena. It started when they were in school together. He seemed to have developed a habit of going to bed late because of studying, which led her to feel that he was taking time away from their relationship. As the years have gone on—decades—since those years of study, the habit never changed and an invisible barrier, what we could probably best describe as lack of intimacy, developed.

Not going to bed together at night might seem like a small thing, but if it is a consistent pattern for many years, it can communicate a major lack of relationship. For this one couple, the husband next began to come home late for supper and told his wife to go ahead and have dinner with the family without him. One by one, the fires of romance and togetherness in their relationship went out. Today she cries out in desperation as a very lonely wife and mother. Little habits make a big difference.

So what to do if you're stuck in the ruts of poor habits that have weakened your relationship? We suggest you write down just two that you'd agree need changing, and work on them for a month. Habits only change by creating new habits. For the man in our example, he could start by planning to meet his wife once a week at a coffee shop for debriefing and time alone. Then he could choose two nights a week that would be sacred for having dinner with his family, also going to bed those nights at the same time as his wife. After that month, the couple should reevaluate to see if a new habit has started. Adjust by either adding more time together to expand the habit, or continuing with the beginning plan until it becomes a way of life. The husband's initiative shows his wife that their relationship is his #1 priority.

Affection Is the Root of Romance

We have yet to meet a woman who does not enjoy romance. In fact, it is safe to say that women crave it. Have you ever met a wife who begged her husband not to waste so much precious time on the unnecessary rituals of romance? You won't. That's what date nights and overnight getaways are all about, and why many women love "chick flicks" that are hopelessly romantic. We have some friends in Chicago who go out to a movie like clockwork every Friday night. One week he picks the movie, and the next week it is her turn. You can probably guess the variety: his night it is *Gladiator,* and for her it is *Notting Hill.* Some other friends in California have every Thursday night as the night the two of them go out to dinner. These tangible dates do communicate affection, which is at the root of romance.

While you are practicing the fine art of dating in marriage, remember the little things like holding hands. Gentle touches mean a great deal to a woman. Touch that conveys your care and pleasure at just being together builds a foundation of closeness in marriage. This kind of touch does not necessarily have the intention of leading to the place a man wants to go: to bed (and we are not talking sleep here).

One young woman wrote this poem to her husband about her tangible need for affection:

Please—
Come take my hand
    Let's walk!!!
Give me your—
    Eyes saying—Hi!
    Glances saying—I care!
    Handholds that let me know that you were only teasing;
    Hugs saying—Thank you for being you!
    Kisses that—gently want me;
Then love—
    That says, I'll be here tomorrow
      and everyday hereafter.
      (*Love Life for Every Married Couple*, Ed Wheat, p. 136).

Dr. Ed Wheat in *Love Life* has this to add about those little touches of affection, like holding hands on a date, like putting your arm around your wife at the movies, and things like toes touching in bed late at night:

> Many couples who build an intense love relationship by caressing while dating often quit affectionate touching after marriage. The reason? Now they are using touch only as a sexual signal to communicate readiness to make love. At other times they carefully stay apart lest an affectionate gesture be misinterpreted.

> Couples must break the habit of using touch exclusively as a signal for sex. This will deprive you of the warmth and physical tenderness that every marriage should have (*Love Live for Every Married Couple*, Ed Wheat, p. 138).

In an earlier chapter we highlighted Johnny Miller, pastor of Calvary Church in Lancaster, Pennsylvania as one of our hero husbands. He is the former president of our alma mater, Columbia International University. As we wind down this chapter (and the book) on keeping the romance alive in marriage, we want to share some of Johnny's powerful words on the meaning of intimacy and it's importance to the human personality:

> When I use the word, "intimacy," I am not thinking primarily of a physical relationship. Unfortunately, that is the only way much of our society understands intimacy. The fact is that two people can have a physical relationship without ever being intimate, and conversely, two people can grow into intimacy without departing into sexuality.
>
> In marriage, the ideal is to have physical oneness that grows out of spiritual and emotional oneness. That is what I mean by intimacy. It is to relate as God meant us to relate in marriage, two people becoming one. It is to be known, and still loved. Marriage provides the ideal conditions to grow in both our exposure and our commitment.
>
> Intimacy is a delightful gift. A vacuum in our personality craves it. It fills the void of loneliness. As God said, "It is not good for man to be alone." If we don't find it with our mate, we'll look for it elsewhere because life is painful without it.
>
> Such soul intimacy is the spring from which family life flows. It makes the family more than a loose collection of individuals spinning off from a common core. Intimacy is a bond of understanding that gives every family member a sense of identity: This is who I am, and I am still loved (From "Intimacy and Bucket Seats." *CIU Quarterly*, Winter 1996).

Hero Husbands We Know

When I was a little boy I remember a movie entitled *Darby O'Gill and the Little People*. Let us tell you about a friend of ours who's great at giving his wife small romantic acts of kindness. We'll call him "Daryl O'Bryan and the Little Romances." Experts tell us that of the various causes of depression among women, one of the most common is the combination of "loneliness, isolation, and boredom" and "an absence of romantic love." Women tend to be more romantic than men, and we men must work hard to constantly practice romance. That is what Daryl does.

What is romantic? Well, flowers are a good possibility, and negligees are romantic. Perfume is very romantic. Giving your wife a card that tells her how much you love her for no special occasion is very romantic. Or leaving her notes around the house to let her know you think about her is romantic. A phone call from work just to tell your wife you are thinking about her definitely scores high in romance.

Not long ago I was in a business meeting with Daryl O'Bryan and noticed his daily planner lying open on the place next to mine. I glanced at the notes he had in the front and saw a most amazing list. On the list were things such as "buy flowers, send a card, make a phone call, surprise her with a dinner out, candlelight, weekend getaways." It was a rather lengthy list, and when I asked him about it, I learned an excellent new technique for all of us men. "Hans," Daryl said to me, "I'm such a dummy when it comes to romance with Mary. You'd think that after being married thirty years I would know how much I need to romance her to keep our marriage alive. I keep this list in front in my daily timer to constantly remind me to do the little acts of romance that will be an encouragement to her. If I don't keep looking at the list, I will just forget, and our marriage will run dry. It's my way of making it and keeping it a priority always before me."

I was so impressed with this approach Daryl took that I have done the same thing and placed it in my calendar. My own list is in Chapter Two on reminding ourselves of a woman's feminine nature.

Putting Principles into Practice

Through the years of our marriage, we've observed that many couples fall into the pattern of concentrating solely on work and childcare. The years when our children were babies and preschoolers were exhausting! I remember wondering if other couples were like us, without the energy or desire to even make love once a month! It was a relief to learn that we were not alone. But we knew it sure wasn't healthy.

So what's the ticket? How do you keep the priority of one another as #1 in your lives? First, talk it over! Set aside a date to talk through what you're both feeling and the desires you have in your relationship that are not being met.

Second, set aside a sacred "date-night" together. Try to plan one night each month for starters. Then if you get really good at it, you might progress to one night a week. Our good friends who are empty nesters find this to be no problem, of course. Since Hans and I never lived near relatives—we have always had to pay a sitter to care for our children. Since it wasn't always easy, sometimes we'd go for an economical dinner or only coffee, but we'd go. Hans has learned that my main desire is to debrief and build

Tim Allen's Top Ten Date Tip

Try Taking Her Shopping at Her Favorite Store to Show Your Love . . . We Guys Know What That Means!

I can't shop with women. I just get tired. I walk into the women's wear department of any store and my energy just goes south. I'm suddenly seven and in the backseat of the family station wagon, being lulled to sleep by the hum of the road.

There's something about fluorescent lights in malls that makes me very weak. It's like they're made of kryptonite. (However, fluorescent lights in electronics stores make me feel suddenly energetic.) Women know this. That's why, instead of letting you go off and do your own shopping, they make you sit in those little student punishment seats by the dressing rooms. Then they waltz out in some . . . frou-frou and say, "What do you think?"

You muster the stock answer. "Nice. Very nice." And then you follow with the appropriate shared "nod and smile" to the exhausted husband in the other chair.

From Tim Allen, *Don't Stand Too Close to a Naked Man*, p. 180.

our relationship. We were thankful when the time finally came for the children to be old enough to take care of themselves.

The applications in this final chapter should seem obvious enough. Men, take the initiative to put romance back into your marriage if you have let it slip away. And remember that you will always need to make your wife feel special by doing those romantic little things you did before you swept her off her feet and won her heart.

Top Tips for Romance:

Date your mate: In the words of Nike, "Just Do It!"

Spend nights away at romantic getaways: Plan your first get-away to a nice hotel or bed and breakfast. Make it a regular part of your annual schedule. It is particularly helpful at the beginning and near the end of each year to look at goals and review your progress as a couple and family.

Write her notes: A wife never tires of getting written notes from her husband. It communicates that you took the time to actually find a card and write something. Get creative and mail it! Leave her notes when you go away on trips that she will discover while you are gone. Send her a romantic or funny card by e-mail.

Spend time away from the children: You are not shirking your responsibility as parents. Both of you and your kids will be better off for it. Remember that the best gift you can give your children is a great marriage.

Find common interests: Do things together that you both enjoy, like biking, tennis, walking, shopping for antiques, or concerts. Common interests make happy memories and alleviate boredom in marriage.

Be sure to change your dating through the seasons of your marriage: Your patterns of dating will obviously change as you go through the cycles of marriage. When the kids are little, you'll need limited objectives unless Grandma and Grandpa are around. Your goal is to have a relationship that is fun and close when the children are finally gone from your nest.

Use outside resources: David and Claudia Arp have a series of excellent seminars, books and resources, including the Marriage Alive Seminar. Contact them through Alive Communications, Colorado Springs, CO, (719) 260-7080.

Also, Cook Communications has partnered with the Lifemates ministry to produce some excellent marriage and dating books: *Lifemates, Dates for Mates,* and *They Call Me Mr. Romance.*

And remember:
All work and no play can make
marriages a very dull place to be.

References Cited

Allen, Tim.
Don't Stand Too Close to a Naked Man, New York:
Hyperion Publishers, 1994.

Barry, Dave.
Dave Barry's complete Guide to Guys, New York:
Random House, 1995.

Dillow, Linda.
Creative Counterpart, Nashville: Thomas Nelson, 1977.

Harley, Willard F., Jr.
His Needs, Her Needs, Grand Rapids: Fleming H. Revell,
1994. Used with permission.

Kennerly, Paul.
"Give a Little Love," (Words and music) 1988 Rondor
Music (London) Ltd. (PRS) Administered by Irving Music,
Inc. (BMI) in U.S.A. and Canada. All rights reserved, used
by permission. WARNER BROS. PUBLICATIONS U.S.
INC., Miami, FL 33014.

Logan, Jim.
Reclaiming Surrendered Ground, Chicago: Moody Press,
1995.

McQuilken, Robertson.
"Muriel's Blessing," *Christianity Today,* February 1996.

Ryan, Ruth.
Covering Home, Waco: Word Books, as quoted on page 87, *Readers Digest,* September 1995.

Smalley, Gary.
If Only He Knew, Grand Rapids: Zondervan, 1982.

Smith, Jim.
Learning to Live with the One You Love, Carol Stream, IL: Tyndale House, 1991. Used with permission.

Swindoll, Charles.
Woman: A Person of Worth and Dignity, Portland, OR: Multnomah Press, 1983.

Tannen, Deborah.
I Only Say This Because I Love You, New York: Random House, 2001.

Walvoord, John F., and Roy Zuck.
The Bible Knowledge Commentary, Colorado Springs: Victor Books, 1989.

Wheat, Ed.
Love Life for Every Married Couple, Grand Rapids: Zondervan, 1980. Used with permission.

Wiersbe, Warren.
Be Rich, Colorado Springs: Victor Books, 1989.

Wright, H. Norman.
Prehysteric Parenting, Colorado Springs: Victor Books, 2001.